This book offers the gift of empathy. A [...] for all blended families, *A Home Built [...] Loss* pays special attention to how loss impacts blended-family bonding. I have been blessed to work with Sabrina McDonald through the years, and you will also be blessed by her candor, insights, and beautifully written testimony of what God can do for your family.

RON DEAL, director of FamilyLife Blended, president of Smart Stepfamilies, and bestselling author of *Building Love Together in Blended Families* (with Gary Chapman) and *The Smart Stepfamily*

Marriage and family are hard work. Period. But unavoidable layers of complexity are added when stepfamilies are formed. Sabrina and Robbie have put in the work to survive the trials after their losses, and today they are thriving and want to help you! Everyone needs a coach, a mentor, and a friend when traveling rough roads. Open these pages and let Sabrina be your companion on your family journey.

DENNIS AND BARBARA RAINEY, cofounders of FamilyLife and authors of thirty-five books, including *Moments Together for Couples* and *The Art of Parenting*

Filled with compassion and biblical wisdom, *A Home Built from Love and Loss* is for those who desire a deeper understanding of the grief associated with blended families. Sabrina McDonald's honest, vulnerable, and inspiring illustrations from her own journey help guide the reader through the complex layers of rebuilding. This resource provides practical steps toward healing and offers hope for today's Christian blended family.

LAURA PETHERBRIDGE, aka "The Smart Stepmom"; speaker, life coach, and coauthor (with Ron Deal) of *The Smart Stepmom*

A Home Built from Love and Loss

A
Home
Built from
Love & Loss

Coming Together as a Blended Family

Sabrina Beasley McDonald

FOCUS
ON THE FAMILY.

*A Focus on the Family resource
published by Tyndale House Publishers*

To Robbie,

my dear husband,

who shares the loss and love with me.

To Benjamin and Katherine,

who delight me continually with laughter.

To Seth,

who endured the brunt

of my learning curve and inspired this book.

Contents

Introduction

WITH EYES GLARING AND JAW CLENCHED, I stood furious and bewildered in front of my new husband, Robbie. Moments before, Robbie had scolded and humiliated my five-year-old son, Benjamin, with the ferocity of a drill sergeant in the first week of training. And it wasn't the first time.

I couldn't understand how Robbie, at the time an Army sergeant, could be so harsh to a child still in kindergarten. Ben's biological father had died three years prior—more than half Ben's life ago—and now Ben was sure his new "daddy" hated him.

Our blended family had only been together for a matter of weeks, maybe a few months, and I was already worried about our future as a family. Would my son and his stepdad ever be able to bond? This kind of turmoil wasn't what I signed up for.

My anger manifested in a whirlwind of emotions. I wasn't sure if I should cry, yell, or take my kids and leave. Nervous energy compelled me to start picking up toys and other living-room debris, taking out my frustration on each stuffed animal and wooden block, snatching them up and flinging them into a laundry basket. I turned my back, refusing to make eye contact with Robbie.

My husband's furrowed brow softened when he saw tears welling in my eyes, blazing with fire as they were. He started with an excuse, "Well, he . . ."

"*He* is in kindergarten," I barked. "*You* are a grown-up."

"What do you want me to do?" Robbie scoffed.

I stopped my furious cleaning, faced him, and—with a look of exasperation—said, "I want you to love my son."

That was the moment I knew that blended-family life was hard, not just "I'll get used to it" hard, but blood, sweat, and tears hard.

The blending of families, it turns out, places parents in deeply emotional situations that sometimes require great sacrifice. Making a stepfamily work requires some of the most difficult decisions a parent can make, yet newly formed stepfamilies face those decisions on an almost daily basis. It's exhausting! So it's no wonder that such a high percentage of stepfamilies end in divorce.

Robbie and I were especially naïve about our coming together as a family. We were both widowed, and we thought our backgrounds would give us an easier and faster path to establishing a strong family connection. But we were wrong, like so many others before us.

When I tell the story of how Robbie and I met, most people respond with a sweet *awww.* Images of *The Sound of*

Music or *The Brady Bunch* come rushing to mind. It seemed so cut and dry: His kids needed a mom; my kids needed a dad. And voilà—everyone has what they need!

The truth is that most couples in a blended family—whether their path led through death or divorce—dream the same naïve dream. Yet the typical stepfamily story is less like *The Brady Bunch* and more like the Montagues and Capulets from *Romeo and Juliet.*

Almost all blended families follow the same basic journey. We start out brimming with hope, but then reality sets in. We realize that marriage didn't fix everything. In fact, some things got much worse. That leads to questions and doubts and, eventually, to the crossroads where all such couples must decide: hang on and keep going, or give up and quit. Those of us who keep going eventually reap the rewards, but not without our scars. And there are always nuances within this journey, of course, because no two families are the same.

There have been times when divorced friends have said to me, "I know I've never lost a spouse, but—" And that's where I stop them. Divorce isn't the same as being widowed, but it's a tremendous loss just the same. It's a loss for the spouse, and it's a loss for the kids. In some ways divorce *is* like death—the death of something (a marriage and family) that you hoped would last a lifetime.

No matter how each stepfamily comes to be, they all include a necessary journey through grief. Loss (and therefore grief) is a factor in every blended family. And even though this process is desperately needed in order to heal, people often overlook the need for grieving when death isn't involved.

Thankfully, as time moved on, Robbie *did* form a bond with my kids. Nowadays it's as if they were always his. My daughter, who was three when we married, doesn't know a life without Robbie in it. I laugh when I see her do something the way Robbie does, or when she plays a trick on him that he taught her. I often say to him, "You know where she got that from, don't you? Her daddy"—meaning Robbie, of course.

It took a while, but I eventually realized that I had expected something in those early years that Robbie couldn't possibly give my children at that time—a bond. That kind of connection doesn't happen just by wishing for it. It takes time and sacrifice.

My family is long past our most vulnerable days, and we are looking forward to a happy future together. But there were many times in our past, like when Robbie scolded Ben, when the future didn't look so good. All stepfamilies go through these moments.

That's because the usual path to blended-family stability is baptism by fire. This wilderness adventure begins with walking across hot coals before moving on to consuming exotic foods like humble pie. Along the way, one can expect the ritual sacrifice of some stubborn habits.

The good news for you is that your family is not the first to travel this path. Other couples, like Robbie and I, have gone before you and can help light the way. That doesn't mean you won't endure your share of scary encounters on this journey, but at least you can be prepared to face them.

This book attempts to explain the trials, tribulations, and triumphs of blending a family. Our story involves a new life that was formed after death, but this book is a resource for any blended family that formed after any number of circumstances. Death, divorce, abandonment, a single parent who was never married, foster care and adoption—these situations and others can be the basis for blending a family.

You might even be a grandparent in a blended family. This group is often overlooked, yet they aren't immune to the issues that affect stepfamilies. The grandparent/grandchild relationship can be a strong emotional bond, so grandparents are often confused and sometimes devastated as they try to determine just where they fit in this blended web of relationships.

Adult children are another overlooked group in the blended-family equation. You might be a grown child who doesn't understand how you fit into your parent's new marriage. Maybe your heart is broken because the only family you've ever known and loved is lost, because a deceased parent seems forgotten, or because the grandparenting dream you had in relation to your kids feels gone forever.

Maybe you have friends or loved ones now struggling in a blended family, or perhaps you are a pastor or small group leader who needs to better understand the dynamics of stepfamilies in your church.

Whatever circumstances prompted you to pick up this book, what you will get is a bag full of tools to help you and others in your circle address the challenges of blended-family life. I'll address topics such as the grief that impacts all blended families, the role of the ex-spouse (whether deceased or alive), changes in family identity for both children and adults, and the beauty that God can bring from the brokenness of life.

Most of all, this book offers the gift of empathy. Through our family's story, you get to take a walk in someone else's shoes. It's hard to gain a thorough perspective if you only see one side of a story, and it's even harder when you are the one who bears the pain, so I hope this book gives you a more complete view of a complex situation.

Suffice it to say that I can't cover every specific situation. Everyone in a stepfamily grieves not just the loss of a former way of life but also the loss of dreams. And they all deal with disappointment, guilt, and a host of frustrations and fears.

Blending a family can be complicated and often deeply emotional, but there is absolutely hope for a fulfilling life. It just takes courage, tenacity, tolerance, and grace, grace, grace.

With a focus on God's Word and a lot of patience for one another, any stepfamily can build a house with a firm foundation. In the next few chapters, I will discuss many distinct issues that stepfamilies face and how they can be dealt with, from both a practical and a biblical perspective.

The stories I'll share don't always represent our most flattering moments. Robbie and I messed up a lot. We hurt feelings a lot. We failed in many ways. But we also fought hard to honor God and maintain a loving home.

If we can do it, so can you.

TWO FUNERALS
AND A WEDDING

OUR WIDOWED DAYS WERE OVER, and Robbie and I couldn't wait to start our new life together.

It had been two years for him and three for me since our spouses died—years of crying, wondering, hoping, and worrying. Those were years of frustrated single parenting and lonely, dismal nights. Our wedding day marked the end of those burdens and an exciting new beginning.

My groom waited for me at the church altar, buttoned up in his military dress blues, and my heart burst like fireworks as I stood ready to walk the aisle. Red roses and navy ribbons adorned the pews along the way where my father would escort me to my new husband-to-be.

When I entered the church sanctuary, I expected bright, beaming faces, joining me in the joy that those lonely, struggling hours were now a distant memory. Instead, I was greeted with a host of red, puffy eyes. Tissues were everywhere as I passed each row. Sniffles echoed. It felt more like a wake than a wedding.

People were happy for us, of course, but they were also deeply saddened. Our wedding was another reminder that their loved ones—our loved ones—were gone.

My first husband, David, and Robbie's first wife, Kari, weren't coming back. It was hard enough for our friends and family to *know* it. It was even harder for them to *see* life changing and moving in a new direction without our beloved departed ones.

It didn't help that our wedding ceremony took place in the same church, in the same room, as Kari's funeral. Robbie's oldest son and daughter-in-law were visibly anxious. She wept throughout the ceremony, and it wasn't just an occasional tear down the cheek, but a shoulders-shaking, trying-to-catch-your-breath kind of cry.

Hers weren't the only tears shed that day. Women on both sides of the aisle couldn't keep their mascara from running.

It was also strange to see David's sister and his widowed mother sitting on the bride's side of the sanctuary. Just ten years earlier, they were on the groom's side.

Robbie's in-laws were on his side. I barely knew them and vice versa. I wondered how their hearts must be breaking. Robbie and Kari were married twenty-two years—high school sweethearts. He was more like a son to them than a son-in-law.

The reception was also awkward. I asked my new teenage stepson to dance, but he didn't feel like it. I understood why. Still, it was hard for me not to feel rejected. I'm sure he didn't know what to feel, especially while so many family members seemed to be in a state of sorrow.

The whole event made me wish we had eloped to the Caribbean. I regretted the cost of this somber affair and longed for a refund on the live band and gourmet food.

When the "party" was over, Robbie and I realized something. This wasn't just a wedding. It was two funerals and a wedding.

We soon realized that each friend and family member was on his or her own grief journey. Our wedding ceremony was just one more step on that long road.

It certainly makes sense to hear the words *grief journey* in the context of death and remarriage, but these same conflicting emotions are also natural when someone who has been divorced gets remarried. That's because this seemingly joyous union signifies the death of the former relationship. In such a case, there are likely those in the family still hoping for the exes to reunite. That's especially true for kids.

No matter how terrible a parent's past behavior—drugs, abuse, infidelity—it's rarely bad enough to dampen the hopes that children have for Mom and Dad to reconcile. Children always—*always*—hope that the "bad" parent will one day be a better person and finally become the hero they always dreamed of.

The grief that occurs when a marriage ends doesn't just hit the children. If you were a part of the marriage, then it also hits you. Yes, I understand that you have probably accepted the end of your marriage—maybe you desperately wanted it to end—but your loss involves more than a *person*. The breakup of a marriage is like the loss of a *dream*—the "happily ever after" dream.

A Match Made Online

I met Robbie on an internet dating site. (How else is a single mother with two preschoolers supposed to meet single men?) I admit that when Robbie first approached me, I wasn't a fan. He was attractive enough, nice enough, and a Christ follower, but our circumstances were completely out of sync. He was ten years older than me, and his kids were much older than mine, with a twenty-year difference between his oldest and my youngest.

Yet the fact that he was widowed gave Robbie and me a sort of camaraderie, like two soldiers who had lived through the same war. For some reason I couldn't stop saying yes to dates with him. He understood a part of me that few others could appreciate.

Something happened one night that helped me realize it was time to stop resisting and give Robbie a chance. I was at a Super Bowl party with a bunch of young singles. I was around thirty-six at the time, and a young man in his early twenties approached me.

As this guy swaggered and chatted with me, it struck me how young he seemed, as if I were talking to a child. Yes, he was only about ten years younger, but it felt like more than that.

Our differences were about more than just age. I had two kids (a maturing process of its own) and had gone through the trauma of losing a spouse. This guy couldn't possibly comprehend any of these experiences, and I didn't expect him to.

That's when I called Robbie and told him to meet me at a restaurant. We sat side by side in a quiet booth and watched the football game together. Nothing much was said, aside from occasionally commenting on a particular play or a funny commercial. It wasn't dramatic or even romantic, but it was comfortable—the way time spent together as a married couple so often is.

The next day I was still pondering. For one thing, I knew that our circumstances weren't ideal. From the outside, our combined family might look crazy. For example, I wasn't old enough to be the mother of the oldest, and Robbie looked more like my kids' grandfather than their father.

Then I looked up on my bathroom wall, and there was the answer. Framed in beautiful calligraphy was 1 Samuel 16:7: "The LORD does not see as man sees; for man looks at the outward appearance, but the LORD looks at the heart" (NKJV).

Robbie's heart was good. He knew God. He studied the Bible. Why would the outward appearance of our family matter if both our hearts were following God?

It reminded me of what my first husband, David, used to say: "A soulmate isn't someone you *find*. It's someone you intentionally and prayerfully *become*." He truly believed (as do I) that any two Christians can marry and have a good marriage as long as they are both following God's Word. When that's the goal of both spouses, virtually any marriage can make it.

If your first marriage ended in divorce, you might be thinking, *I was married to a Christian and we still didn't make it*. Being married to a Christian isn't the magic formula for a good marriage. Christian people still choose to sin and live according to the flesh. A *flourishing* marriage, however, involves both spouses desiring God's will and doing their best to follow His guidance and wisdom. When a marriage between two Christians fails, it could be because at least one partner wasn't living a life that was pleasing to God.

If you've now started over—or are about to start over—then your new marriage certainly has the potential to flourish. But it doesn't happen without work. A healthy Christian marriage requires that you both seek and follow God's principles. That's no guarantee that you'll never disagree, but it is a recipe for inner peace and joy.

I Was Ruth. She Was Naomi.

I reached the point where I had just about decided that Robbie was the man God provided for me and my children. (Robbie had actually made up his mind long before.) But there was one person whose opinion mattered to me most—a person whose approval I wanted before I could proceed any further. That person was David's mother, Joy.

If you're in a blended family, you know that your previous spouse's parents don't simply go away. They are still the grandparents of your children, and they still want to spend time with them. Their child is no longer alive to look out for their interests, so it's up to the surviving spouse to include the in-laws in the children's lives.

Oddly enough, David's mother had walked the same path of widowhood as I did. The similarities are almost eerie. Joy's husband, like mine, was killed in a car accident when her children were young. David was two years old at the time and her daughter was only a baby, just like my daughter.

But for whatever reason, Joy never remarried. That was the biggest regret of her life, but not because she regretted her lack of companionship. She was perfectly content living without a husband, but she regretted it for the sake of her children.

Both David and his sister, Jerra, became well-adjusted adults, but David never got over growing up without a father. He often told me, "If anything ever happens to me, promise me you will get married again." To which I would say, "Yeah, yeah, whatever you want. What are the odds?"

When David died, Joy had a similar request of me. She said, "Don't do what I did. Get married again."

In my mind, Joy and I were like Ruth and Naomi: both widowed, both lost, and both in search of a Boaz—a "kinsman redeemer" (in our case, a brother in Christ) who would serve as the man in our lives. (You can read their story in the book of Ruth.) Of course God doesn't promise every single parent a new spouse, much less one of Boaz's reputation and stature. Simply dating as a single parent is already tough enough without the pressure to find that ideal person. And that's before the work of *blending* has even begun!

Joy and Jerra felt responsible to help fulfill David's wishes, to help me find a new spouse. During my three years of widowhood, those two set me up with four different men.

One was a young man who rescued Joy when her car broke down on the highway. She was smitten! Joy made me go with her to visit his church the next Sunday. Unfortunately, his fiancée was a little perturbed to see us show up in person to thank him for being a knight in shining armor!

When it came time to introduce Robbie to Joy, I was nervous. In a way, I felt like she was a stand-in for David—the one destined to give me the "family blessing" so to speak. I knew her opinion would help seal the deal for me, one way or the other. Joy had high standards for just about everything, and my relationship with Robbie had some, shall we say, structural concerns.

I previously mentioned our children's ages. But then there were *our* ages. As I said, I'm ten years younger than Robbie. I'm also only twelve years older than his oldest son, who happens to be about the same age as my youngest brother. Robbie was the youngest of three children, so his sisters and their husbands are closer in age to my parents than to me.

I had already struggled through many of these issues, but what would Joy think?

Joy and Robbie met at my house, and the two of them sat on the back patio to talk. I played inside with the kids, glancing out the window from time to time, trying to judge their expressions. To this day I still don't know all that was said.

Robbie went home and I sat at the kitchen table, waiting to hear Joy's verdict. In my heart, she would render the final ruling. She was the one who would reveal whether Robbie was the man we were waiting for. Was he our Boaz, our provision, from God?

What she said in that moment amazed me. Not only was Joy known for her high standards, she was also known to be somewhat reserved in sharing her opinions. But not that day. It almost felt like a word from the Lord because she spoke with such strength and authority.

"Sabrina, I am so impressed," she said. "I was afraid you would fall in love with a man who wasn't right for you, but I want to tell you something: *You* did not find Robbie; *God* brought you together. He is kind and respectful and mature. He is a blessing from God, and it's no accident that you met. He is perfect for the family, and I feel that I can love him like I loved my own son."

That's when I knew Robbie was the one.

A Grief Journey for the Whole Family

Robbie and I initially bonded over our shared experience with sudden loss. His wife, Kari, died at forty-two of an aggressive form of cancer. The disease was discovered in her spine in May, and by July she entered the gates of heaven. Even though the family could see it coming, it still happened too quickly to absorb.

Surviving family members of cancer victims can sometimes work through much of their grief before the person dies. But Kari's decline was so rapid, there was little time to consider a future without her. Robbie was left being a single father of twelve- and twenty-two-year-old sons, both of whom were experiencing important stages of transition in life.

My husband, David, died instantly in a car accident at the age of thirty-seven. He left for work one morning and never came home. An eighteen-wheeler was making an illegal pass across a double yellow line and struck my husband's car head-on. His car spun around and hit another vehicle. Traffic was backed up for miles and blocked the highway for hours.

Our son was only two and our daughter was three months old when their father drew his last breath.

As devastating as those losses were for Robbie and me, we weren't the only ones who suffered. Our children, parents, in-laws, brothers and sisters, friends, and even distant family members all shared in our pain.

I think we instinctively knew that others were hurting, but we didn't recognize how deep that sorrow ran until we got engaged. It's hard to pay attention to someone else's agony when the biggest yearning in your life is to put an end to your own.

In hindsight, we gave our friends and family little time to

adjust to the idea of a remarriage. I was shocked and somewhat hurt when my family and friends urged that we "slow down" and "get to know each other better."

They didn't say those things back when David and I got engaged. I didn't realize at the time that their desire for Robbie and me to slow down wasn't simply out of concern for our relationship. It also had to do with *everyone else's* need to process what was happening.

Robbie and I married only six months after we met—a mistake we regret to this day. Our rushed relationship wasn't bad for us, per se, but it seemed to make things harder for both our families.

In the minds of our loved ones, Robbie and I were total strangers, and in some ways we were. I had met Robbie's two sons, Will and Seth, only a couple of times before our wedding day. And Robbie had just a few opportunities to interact with my two small children, Benjamin and Katherine.

We thought getting married as soon as possible would be best for the kids. I don't know why we thought that. Wishful thinking, maybe? I had read all the books by blended-family expert Ron Deal, including *Dating and the Single Parent*, that explain why it's best to date at least two years before a second marriage.[1] I should have known better.

But Deal did offer a caveat that "maybe" marriage could come sooner for couples with younger kids, if only because they tended to bond faster. That was all the permission we needed. We heard what we wanted to hear. Benjamin was five and Katherine was three when we made the decision.

Clearly we would be candidates for fast bonding . . . or so we thought.

Robbie and I started dating in January. By spring we were engaged. We really wanted to wait a little longer, but Robbie's son Seth was entering ninth grade—high school. And my son, Ben, would be starting kindergarten.

Since marriage would involve at least one of us moving to a new city, we decided to get married in the summer so the kids wouldn't have to change schools mid-year. So that's what we did.

Looking back, I realize that we somehow expected our new marriage to fix our friends' and families' pain and sorrow. Perhaps the same way I hoped it would fix mine. After all, each person I talked to was eager for me to remarry, and they all approved of Robbie, even if the pace of our relationship was too fast for most. I thought my friends and family members would be relieved for my sake, knowing I had a good man to help provide for my safety, my kids, and my happiness. And in many ways, they were.

But what I didn't realize, and they probably didn't either, was that the lingering sadness of David's loss would not be assuaged by another marriage.

Not only that, but another marriage created a host of new concerns for everyone involved. The grandparents wondered if the children would be properly loved. Friends and family members wondered if the deceased would be forgotten. Robbie and I wondered all those things and more.

Blending our families didn't mean our grief was ending.

It simply meant that our grief was entering a new phase. And that's true for all blended families, no matter how they came to be.

We're Here to Stay

If I had it to do over again, I'd do several things differently. I've already said that I would wait longer before marrying, and there are other issues I would have worked through during that time.

I would have made sure that Robbie's sons, Seth and Will, were more included in his plans. I would have looked for ways to bond with Robbie other than over the loss of our spouses. I would have had all our kids spend more time together.

It's impossible to know how things might be different had we taken these steps, but I do think it would have sent a message to our children and our loved ones: We care about your feelings on the matter, not just our own.

Second thoughts, however, don't change circumstances. We are where we are, and we're here to stay.

And so are you.

Blended families come to be in countless different ways. Maybe you lost a spouse after an affair, or even multiple affairs. Maybe you were the one who was unfaithful. Maybe your spouse was depressed and just left.

Maybe you're worried that getting remarried was the biggest mistake of your life, and now you're questioning whether it can be undone. But whatever the difficulties you experienced, or even created, they are all *redeemable* in the hands of God.

One of my hobbies is upcycling. (Unlike typical recycling, upcycling involves giving new life to items you might otherwise throw away.) I love to take old stuff and make something new out of it. With a little glue, paint, and imagination, I try to create beauty out of items that have been cast away and forgotten.

That's also one of God's specialties. How do I know? Look at Moses—a tongue-tied killer whom God trusted with His Law. Look at Gideon's army—a cast of 300 men who took on the entire Midianite army. Look at the ragtag group of twelve disciples whom the Lord used to help bring His gospel to the whole world!

I often say that God likes to use people and situations that look hopeless because no one else can take credit when He makes something amazing out of almost nothing. When people hear stories like that, they have to say, "Only God could have done this!"

In the same way, when you trust God with your stepfamily, He can bring about something beautiful—even when others might have given up. As Philippians 1:6 says, "He who began a good work in you will bring it to completion at the day of Jesus Christ." As tempting as it might be at times, don't give up on your new family. Allow God to finish His work. It might look like your blended family is a mishmash of discarded items. But when God gets done with it, you'll stand back in awe and say, "Only God could have done this."

LOSS IN DEATH,
LOSS IN REMARRIAGE

WHEN I FIRST MET ROBBIE, his oldest son, Will, was engaged and basically on his own. But Robbie's teenage son, Seth, still lived with Robbie at home.

Robbie and Seth were like two bachelors living the good life, watching football and basketball on television and going out to eat whenever they wanted.

I remember visiting one night after Robbie and I were engaged. I surveyed the atmosphere in the living room. The lights were low. Noise muted. They both sat back in their reclining chairs, casually discussing the latest game while surfing their phones.

I mused over how different their lives would be in a

few short weeks, when they were sharing a home with two rambunctious, attention-seeking preschoolers. I giggled to myself, wondering how they thought they were going to pull off this peaceful evening atmosphere at my house.

"You know . . . this quiet bachelor lifestyle is going away after you marry me, right?" I confessed to Robbie privately.

"I know," he said. "It'll be fine."

Maybe he believed that when he said it. But it wasn't long after our wedding that he stopped believing it.

I, on the other hand, was happily kissing single-mom life good-bye and thanking God for bringing a man into our lives. I looked forward to Robbie's parenting help with my kids—especially Benjamin, who would benefit from discipline and mentoring from a man. And I wistfully looked forward to Robbie and Seth helping with chores. I just knew that Robbie would help me carry the heavy burdens that I'd borne by myself for so long, and Seth would surely be a big help to his new little brother and sister.

I had expected *some* mishaps and maladjustment. I knew the two bachelors would have to get used to the pitter-patter of little feet. I wasn't sure how Seth would take to living with little kids, and I guessed that my children might be apprehensive of the two strange men they would soon call "Dad" and "Brother."

But Seth had such an upbeat personality that I was hopeful he would slide into his new big-brother role with ease. All in all, Robbie and I thought everyone would catch on fairly quickly and get along.

Wrong, wrong, aaand wrong.

It took only a few weeks of living together as a family to learn that our expectations were *way* too high.

We discovered that our emotional hurts weren't behind us just because we were now married. What's more, our new family would create even more reasons to grieve.

The Role of Grief in Blended Families

Death, of course, is one reason for grief, but there are countless other reasons. At its most basic level, grief is the deep disappointment that occurs when future dreams and aspirations (even small ones) are forever taken away with no hope of returning.

Some might even liken grief to a feeling of betrayal. Perhaps you feel like God was leading you down a path of blessing, only to take it all away. Maybe you feel tricked, mocked, or forgotten. And it all leads to that single, ever-present question: Why?

Why did this happen? Why did my husband die? Why did my wife leave?

Grief involves losses of the past, present, and future—haunting memories, guilt from previous decisions, fears of the unknown. All kinds of losses (or perceived losses) can lead to grief, especially when things are new, unstable, and chaotic.

It's hard enough to navigate this emotional maze as a single parent. Most of us hope a new marriage will bring a fresh new start, but remarriage often compounds the emotions that already existed. The added grief experienced by blended families is what I call "double grief." Memories that seemed long forgotten can reappear, and new fears can form, especially for children:

- "Does my parent still love me as much as before?"
- "My new stepparent seems harsh. Does he/she even like me?"
- "How could I love someone who is trying to replace my real parent?"

Let me give you some examples of the double grief that my family faced when we all moved in together.

Robbie and I decided it was best that he and Seth move into my house with my kids. It was the logical choice because my house had enough bedrooms for everyone and it was closer to my son's school. So Robbie and Seth had to put their furniture, dishes, and other personal items that we didn't need in storage. That meant all the familiar surroundings from their home were gone, replaced by mostly my things. That seemingly minor decision made Robbie and Seth feel like they were living in "my" house, not "our" house.

Robbie and Seth also had to move to my city, about thirty-five minutes from where they lived before. That also meant Seth had to change schools. This change turned out to be positive in the long run, but Seth had to make a whole new set of friends and learn the new school's curriculum. He had to navigate being the "new guy." Both home *and* school were now alien landscapes.

The changes didn't affect only Robbie and Seth. My little ones did not bond with their new family members like we thought—and hoped—they would. I watched helplessly as my five-year-old cried about his new dad, whom he wished would go away. The woman my son loved (me) was now sharing her life with another person (Robbie).

And remember all that help around the house that I naïvely expected? Well, Robbie didn't require Seth to do any chores. And since Robbie felt like they were living in "my" house, he somehow thought of helping as intruding. I'm sure you can guess how that made me feel.

I could list probably a hundred different examples of expectations and hurt feelings that we all endured during those early years. And I can list another hundred that we still experience all these years later—not as regularly, perhaps, but often.

The truth is, as stepfamilies change and grow, there will always be new griefs and issues. But isn't that true for all families?

Blended families often get a bad rap, but whether biologically related or not, we're all imperfect humans living with other imperfect humans. Life isn't a fairy tale, and grief occurs naturally in all families. So rather than trying to avoid grief, why not embrace it and all the good it brings?

Wait . . . did I just say that grief can be good?

Good Grief

When I talk about grief, most people get a bit antsy. After all, grief can be scary. Awkward. Yet grief can also be a valuable tool.

After my husband David died, I used to say, "I wish no one ever had to go through this—and at the same time, I wish everyone had to go through this."

I've learned that there are some physical benefits to grief. The most commonly cited stages of the grieving process—denial, anger, bargaining, depression, and acceptance—can also serve as coping mechanisms for the devastating losses we encounter in life.

For example, crying is a form of relief. It releases chemicals that calm the body. In a similar way, someone in shock gets a momentary time-out from thinking and feeling, giving the brain a chance to slowly accept reality. Anger allows us to express pent-up frustration, and bargaining helps us sort out the truth when the spiritual and physical realities of deep loss collide.

Healing is much harder without these coping mechanisms. We run the risk of losing hope and eventually becoming so dark and calloused that we care for no one, not even ourselves.

Even though we need these processes to heal, we live in a world that is afraid of sadness. Concerned friends try to "rescue" us from the grieving process. When a child cries, we feel compelled to say, "Don't cry. It's going to be okay." Many young men have been raised to believe that "real men don't cry." Young children insult each other over sadness, saying, "Don't be a baby."

Sorrow makes people feel uncomfortable, so they want to make it stop. They want to make it go away.

In the book *Don't Take My Grief Away*, there's a story of a woman who lost her baby to a sudden illness. As you can imagine, the woman cried and screamed hysterically, and people tried to calm her down. With eyes of fire, she demanded, "Don't take my grief from me. I deserve it. I am going to have it."[1]

I identified with this woman's desperate plea. When my husband died, a well-meaning friend visited with intentions to "get my mind off the death."

Her heart was in the right place. I know that. But she couldn't understand that getting my mind off David's death was impossible! It defined my entire life at that time. I *needed* to talk about it because my mind was swirling, trying to understand what life meant to me now.

On top of that, I process best through language, so talking about David's death was my way of working through it. I remember the anguish of not being "allowed" to talk about my pain in our conversation. Talking about it was all I had!

After I read the story of the bereaved mother and considered my own experience, I wondered how many times in the past I had tried to take grief away from others. How many times had I denied someone the right to grieve in my presence because it was uncomfortable to me? How many times had I filled the air with philosophical jargon? How many times had I tried to explain away someone else's tragedy?

Just the other day my daughter, Katherine, was devastated by a thoughtless offense from some friends. From an adult perspective, I knew this was short-lived and probably the result of a girlish misunderstanding. So while she wept from a broken heart, I was rationalizing the problem. I said things such as "This will all work itself out," "Don't worry about it," and "No need to cry about it."

At first she was frustrated, struggling to explain to me why her grief *was* justified. Then I felt her put up a wall between us. She said, "Whatever, mom. You just don't understand."

The more I rationalized, the more she shut me out.

To her it was obvious that I didn't understand and didn't *want* to understand. I finally caught myself and immediately stopped rationalizing. I said, "Katherine, I am so sorry, sweetie. I know how bad it feels to be hurt by a friend. There's hardly anything that feels worse than that."

That was what she needed to hear all along. My empathy. Her countenance softened and she leaned her head on my shoulder. Not only did my acceptance of her pain make her feel better, but it drew her closer to me.

What was my motive for pushing my "logic" on her? I really don't know. It's almost as if I believed empathy would encourage her to wallow in sadness, keeping her stuck there. But in reality, the opposite was true.

Many people who go through a divorce experience this

kind of consolation from their friends. They say things like "Good riddance. You didn't need him anyway." Or "Why aren't you happy? Didn't you want this?"

Friends and family members don't seem to realize that even "necessary" divorces are heartbreaking. You once loved this person. You once had dreams of a happy ending. Maybe you had children together and you imagined one day sitting together watching the grandkids play. Those hopes seem gone forever.

It's not really a question of whether you wanted the divorce. Few people really *want* a divorce. What we want is to have a healthy, trustworthy spouse who loves us unconditionally and lives a decent life. But everyone makes choices, sometimes bad ones, and divorce is sometimes the result.

Could the end of an abusive marriage be a reason to rejoice? Yes, we are relieved that the abuse or infidelity is over. But that same situation is also a reason to mourn. The hope of restoration is gone. Thankfully, we don't have to choose one emotion over the other. We can feel both at the same time, and that includes the sorrow.

"I Don't Deserve to Grieve"

When I lost David, several divorced friends expressed how they experienced similar feelings after their marriage ended. Then they would quickly apologize, saying something like "I don't mean to compare my loss to yours. I know death is much harder than divorce."

But is that always the case? Is the end of a marriage

through death or through an unwanted divorce really that much different? I'm not sure. It seems to me divorce is almost like a living death.

My pain isn't necessarily worse than everyone else's. Yes, my spouse is no longer with me, but I don't have to see him love someone else. I don't have to run into him in public. I don't have to question my failings in the relationship and ask myself all the what-ifs.

Divorced people also often seem to have a kind of guilt about grieving. It's as if they feel they don't meet the criteria or don't deserve it. I hear things like "I don't know why I'm sad. It's what I wanted." Or "I guess God will never bless my stepfamily."

A divorced friend once confided to me how she couldn't understand her feelings of depression now that her marriage was over. Her ex-husband was verbally and sometimes physically abusive. She certainly didn't want him in her life anymore.

When I questioned whether her depression was actually unresolved grief, she scoffed, "I don't even like him. I'm not sorry he's gone."

I explained that she wasn't grieving the loss of the *person*. She was grieving the loss of her dreams. She'd lost the "happily ever after" that she dreamed about from the time she was a little girl. She was grieving the disappointment of her love story ending in tragedy, like crying at the end of a heartbreaking movie.

If you're a remarried widow, you might feel like you aren't

allowed to grieve because people will judge your new marriage. You think sorrow might reflect badly on your current spouse. People may think, *If she was really happy in her new marriage, then she wouldn't miss her previous spouse so much. I wonder what's wrong.* What they don't understand is that a person can be happy and sad at the same time.

After David died, I remember thinking, *Would he want me to cry? Maybe not. But he was too good of a man not to cry over.* I wanted the whole world to see my pain because I wanted them to know the great depth of my loss.

Those who hold back the tears see their stoicism as a type of penance. They keep the pain inside and try to suppress the feelings of loss, like their sorrow somehow isn't valid.

The result is that they can't recover. Their wounds remain irritated, only closing up for a moment before reopening again. They refuse to allow the feelings of grief and loss to do their healing work.

Grief after Remarriage

A person who remarries doesn't expect their grief to follow them into the new relationship. Dating provides the temporary euphoria of falling in love again, and it is a powerful painkiller. And those who don't recognize their grief for what it is tend to also misunderstand the cure. They think if they can fall in love with just the right person, then all will be well. When they discover that even the right person won't fix their emotions, the grief eventually returns.

I remember seeing a lack of grief in Robbie when I was dating him, and that was a concern. I knew he was probably dating me to help keep those feelings at bay. I also figured that if I decided to marry him, I would need to help him work through his grief. Turns out I was right. Sometimes he took out his feelings on me, and sometimes he took them out on the kids. Sometimes he would blame his emotions on work or being tired, but I knew what the issue really was. Looking back now, he recognizes it too.

Some feelings of grief will stay with you for the rest of your life, and letting go of the rest can take much longer than most anticipate. One thing is for sure—it doesn't magically go away after remarriage. That's one of the reasons why so many second marriages end in second divorces.

It's important to take a step back when things get tense in your blended family. Take time to evaluate your own fears, sorrows, and grievances. When you can pause and view everyone in your family through the eyes of Christ, you can better identify with their sorrows. This simple exercise in empathy can strengthen bonds and help heal wounds with the members of your blended family.

The Compassionate Christ

Christians aren't always the best when it comes to expressing empathy because we want everyone to be healthy and whole. We don't like to see hurting people. We want to see them *healed*.

One problem is that most of us don't realize expressing grief is part of the healing process. It's hard to understand how encouraging someone to cry is healthy and restorative. But Jesus modeled this very process after the death of His dear friend Lazarus.

In John 11, Jesus received word that Lazarus was ill. But Jesus purposely stayed where He was until Lazarus had died. It was all part of Jesus' plan to raise Lazarus from the dead and thereby glorify God.

By the time Jesus arrived at the tomb, Lazarus had already been dead for four days. People stood nearby weeping and mourning his death, not knowing what was about to take place.

But instead of scolding the group for their lack of faith, Jesus shows a powerful display of compassion. This is what the Bible says happened moments before Jesus raised Lazarus from the dead:

> When Jesus saw [Lazarus's sister Mary] weeping, and the Jews who had come with her also weeping, he was deeply moved in his spirit and greatly troubled. And he said, "Where have you laid him?" They said to him, "Lord, come and see." Jesus wept. So the Jews said, "See how he loved him!" (John 11:33-36)

Did you catch that? Jesus cried with the others. He didn't chastise the people for their lack of faith. He shared in their grief!

Even though Jesus knew He was about to raise Lazarus

from the dead and perform one of the greatest miracles of His ministry, He still wept because He was "deeply moved in his spirit and greatly troubled." He mourned with the mourners. How compassionate our Lord is!

If Jesus wept for those who were overcome with grief, shouldn't we also empathize with the pain of others?

Jesus wasn't the only person in the Bible to show sadness. Yvonne Ortega, author of *Moving from Broken to Beautiful Through Grief*, searched the Scriptures and found seventy-seven instances that mentioned various people crying.[2]

I'm convinced that some who struggle with depression have never felt the freedom to weep and mourn. Thus, their grief remains bound up in their hearts, making them perpetually soul sick. We need to encourage others not to fear their sadness but to embrace it. And sometimes we need to join them in their sorrow. That includes the members of your own blended family.

Grief in Disguise

I've often said that the death of a spouse is like having your arm cut off, but divorce is like having your arm *torn* off. Either way, the result is the same: Your arm is gone, and it's not coming back. There is no way to replace what was lost. But you can learn how to live, and even thrive, in a new way, just as our family has done.

While a person who loses an arm can usually learn to drive again, to write again, and to eventually carry on as well as many people with two arms, the person who loses an arm never gets to the point of saying, "I'm so glad I don't have that arm anymore. Life is better without it." That would sound bizarre! Yet when it comes to losing a marriage, others want to hear that you have moved on and that life is better now.

Losing a spouse, no matter how that person was lost, is not that much different than losing a limb. Yes, I did find love again. Yes, I can be happy and move on with my life. Yet I still miss the relationship I lost and the future we never had.

I still have dreams about David, and sometimes I wake up remembering how much fun he was to be around. Other times I'll see someone on a crowded street with his same build and it makes me do a double take. It's almost like my mind is still subconsciously looking for him. Just hearing a familiar song brings back memories.

I can see traces of his smile on my daughter's face, and his quirky habits in my son. Nurture plays a big role in raising a child, but nature cannot be denied. Their father's DNA is ever present in my kids.

Robbie, meanwhile, notices women with distinctive, curly red hair like Kari's. And thanks (or, in some cases, no thanks) to Facebook, memories of Kari pop up on his timeline that take him back to the moment when the picture was taken.

Those are the moments when grief is readily apparent. But there are also times when grief shows up and it's not so obvious. It can manifest in ways that are hard to recognize in both adults and children. It's what I refer to as "grief in disguise."

It might appear in the form of bad behavior, frustration,

anger, depression, or anxiety. All kinds of mental health issues can arise from unprocessed grief. Children are especially vulnerable to this, but it also affects adults—even those who think they've already worked through their grief.

When Robbie retired after thirty-two years in the military, he went through a serious time of depression. He no longer had his same purpose nor a daily schedule to distract him from his grief, and the emotions hit him hard and without warning.

It had been nearly ten years since Kari's death, and now he was facing life after retirement—the future they'd dreamed about—without her. The sadness was overwhelming.

He remembered the plans they'd made, the trips they would have taken, and how proud Kari would have been of their grandbaby. Their two boys were grown by the time Robbie retired, and he and his high school sweetheart would have been footloose and fancy-free! And it would have been for the first time in their lives since they married so young and had a child right away.

But she was no longer around to enjoy the fruits of their labor.

Robbie has now watched both their sons get married without Kari. He's seen the birth of his first grandchild without her. When Robbie retired, Kari wasn't there to accept her military-wife award—the Army's way of thanking a wife for her sacrifices throughout her husband's service.

This same kind of grief in disguise can also happen after divorce and remarriage. Following the birth of a grandchild, you might resent the idea that your ex's new spouse is also considered a grandparent. You might even wonder why your ex treats the new spouse with more respect or kindness than you received when the two of you were still married.

I know a couple who divorced because the woman wanted to live near a certain city where her children and grandchildren were. The man wanted to live further away because of certain allergies. They couldn't reach a compromise, and the marriage ended.

Then the woman started hearing from friends that he was still hanging around that certain city, even after their divorce. She was devastated. "If he had just done this while we were married," she told me, "we could still be together!" Her questions consumed her.

Grief in disguise sometimes appears for seemingly no reason at all. It's like a ninja jumped out from around a corner and kicked you in the face. You have no idea who was behind the mask or why it happened. All you know is that it hurts like the dickens. You want to cry, get mad, get revenge, and curl up in a ball—all at the same time!

But you'll never get back at the ninja, so you either take out your frustration on your family, or you take the time to examine your feelings and work through the pain.

If you don't work through the pain, grief can manifest itself in affairs, substance abuse, angry outbursts, physical abuse, severe anxiety, or depression. These are life-altering conditions that can destroy otherwise healthy relationships.

If you find yourself struggling with any of these problems, don't ignore it. Talk to a pastor or Christian counselor. Work through a Bible study on grief to help you process your emotions. Find a safe space where you can express your sadness, and don't be afraid to explore the dark depths of your feelings.

Grief upon Grief

The grief of a marriage ending is profound, but forming a new blended family often leads to its own forms of grief. These are largely unavoidable simply based on the process of uprooting one's home, disrupting the foundation, and grafting it into another home.

Likely everyone in the family has already endured a giant heartache of brokenness. Take, for example, a teenage girl who is grieving the breakup of a dating relationship. To her it feels like the world is ending. Now imagine that this same girl always went to her mother for relationship help in the past, but her mom isn't around anymore.

Who should I talk to? she wonders. *Who would care as much as Mom?* The girl might wonder if God has abandoned her. She might wonder if God is not so good after all but is mean and vindictive. Yet she doesn't share her questions with anyone for fear that they won't understand or might shame her for feeling this way.

So that's three losses in one. She lost her boyfriend. Her mother and confidant is gone. And now her relationship with God has become distant.

When a marriage ends, whether through divorce or death, each member of the family must deal with the loss of a spouse or parent, at least to a certain degree. The creation of a blended family, meanwhile, brings with it a whole new batch of physical and emotional upheavals.

Holiday traditions change. Birth orders change. Moving to a new home can lead to the loss of classmates, teachers, or church community. Some of these people might have been pillars of strength in a child's life as he or she endured the loss of a parent or the trauma of divorce.

"Kids are resilient," we are told. And they are, but only to a degree. They absolutely need help working through their grief, just like adults. But because we think kids are so resilient, a child's grief is often overlooked or ignored. The result is that the kids end up bringing their unresolved emotions into the stepfamily.

Children need stability, so when family life is disrupted, they don't understand their feelings or how to cope with the emotional strain. That kind of profound loss can alter the course of their life, sometimes in bad ways. This seems to be especially true for teenagers.

Teenagers might rebel, act out in school, or suffer from depression. Younger children might throw fits, bully other kids, or have a hard time paying attention in class.

My son, Ben, started kindergarten just a few weeks after Robbie and I got married. I had no idea what was going on with him at the time, but looking back, I can see that he was suffering from the stress of our new blended-family life.

I thought a child that young would cope well with creating a stepfamily, but that was not the case. Ben's teachers wondered if he had ADHD. He seemed to live in la-la land through much of the day and forget simple instructions, and at home he would have fits of rage. Yet as our new family life became more stabilized, Ben was better able to handle both school and home.

In addition to the need for stability, another issue for kids is the new set of relationships in a blended family. Anytime new relationships are formed there is going to be tension. That's human nature. But children have a hard time navigating the complexities of those relationships, especially ones with adults.

Parenting styles and personalities will clash. What is considered normal in one family is extreme in another. For example, I was used to raising my voice when I got mad. My young kids rolled with it and brushed it off. They didn't take it personally because they were used to my behavior. To them it was normal. But Robbie's son Seth wasn't used to it. He thought I was a crazy person.

Robbie, meanwhile, was used to grabbing his kids by the arm in a heated discussion in order to get their attention. Well, he certainly got my kids' attention. They thought Robbie was going to maim them!

Influences from outside the family can create tension too. Friends and loved ones can be suspicious of new relationships that seem to be progressing too quickly, especially if one half of the relationship is wealthy, popular, or easily taken advantage of.

Sadly, those suspicions aren't always unfounded. One widowed man I know was so lonely after the death of his first wife that he remarried very quickly to a younger woman. After they wed, his new bride quit her job and convinced him to spend all his savings on an investment opportunity. The investment failed, and she divorced him shortly thereafter.

While these kinds of tragedies do happen, it's still hard to know there are family members who look on your new marriage with suspicion. It's even harder when you know there are those who hope you fail, those who point out your mistakes to the family, and those who gossip behind your back.

Then there is the influence of the previous spouse on the new stepfamily. It doesn't matter whether your blended family was formed after death or divorce, there often remains a strong bond of loyalty to the biological parent, especially among the kids. And depending on how the previous spouse handled the divorce or impending death, he or she could have made comments or asked for promises that can influence the forming of the new family.

In the case of impending death from illness or disease, there are often promises made to the dying person that forever alter the family's future.

In my case, David didn't know he was going to die, but he said something once that gave me peace. He made me promise that if anything ever happened to him, I would get married again so that our kids would have a daddy.

So many times, when I watch the kids achieve a certain milestone or make me incredibly proud, I feel a twinge of sadness knowing that David should be the one seeing it with me. But then his words come back to me, and I am comforted knowing that David wouldn't be sad or jealous that someone else was raising his kids. He'd be pleased that they have a daddy.

I know another widowed woman whose husband was dying. On his deathbed, the husband made her promise that she *wouldn't* get married again. He said he couldn't stand to think of her married to someone else.

She made the promise. Then she broke the promise. She eventually married again, and I asked her how she made that decision. "He needed peace," she said, "and I couldn't take that from him, even though I knew I might break the promise."

I asked her if she ever felt bad about it. "Yes," she replied, "but I did what I had to do."

Now imagine if that same man had asked his kids to never love another daddy. Imagine how much guilt would follow those children into a blended family—especially if the kids *wanted* to love a stepfather. One wonders if they would ever recognize that not all promises are good and some are even unhealthy.

This scenario isn't limited to situations where a parent has died. It happens all the time within stepfamilies after a divorce. Biological parents get jealous of stepparents, and kids end up stuck in the middle. Even statements as seemingly innocent as "Will you always love me?" or "Will you ever forget me?" can make children feel guilty for loving the stepparent in their lives. It can feel like an act of betrayal to the parent they loved first.

There are all sorts of ways that emotions pressure a blended family. We might be tempted to think that it would be easier to simply give up. But that's not the answer.

God is not surprised by your circumstances. He's not wringing His hands wondering how you're going to get through this. In fact, He has provided a way.

The Bible Tells Me So

Someone recently said to me, "The church doesn't have a good theology for suffering." Even though the Bible is well stocked with passages about handling grief and suffering, the best many churches can do is muster the "casserole brigade," as my father-in-law calls it. In other words: food and visits.

Don't get me wrong. It's great that churches know how to take care of physical needs. As a single mom I am eternally grateful for the help I received from the body of Christ after my first husband died. I had meals for months. Our lawn was more beautiful than David ever kept it. A group of friends even started a college fund for my kids.

Unfortunately, most churches aren't quite as good at caring for single parents who ended up single after divorce, even though those parents need that care just as much.

And while most church folks are great at bringing food, they typically aren't as good at "weeping with those who weep" (Romans 12:15). Just like most everyone else, they want to see everyone happy. They want to either hide from grief or fix it. "God has a plan for you," they told me. "And don't worry. You'll get married again."

Well, I already knew that God had a plan. That doesn't mean I had to *like* it! And I didn't want to get married again; I wanted to be married to *David*!

The greatest comfort I received was from those friends and loved ones who missed David with me. They cried with me and shared in my pain. Their tears validated to me that David was worth missing. They validated that I wasn't over-reacting or simply being dramatic. Their tears were like warm oil poured over my soul.

Making Space for Sorrow

The point of these lessons about grief isn't to provide a judgment on how churches should deal with grief. The point is that you need to deal with the grief in your *family*. Everyone in your blended family is grieving. The question is not *if* they are grieving, but rather *how* they are grieving.

If you want to love the people in your home well, if you want peace in your stepfamily, if you want to earn the trust of your stepchildren and your new spouse, you need to create space for them to express sorrow. They can't experience healing unless and until they've processed their emotions.

That said, sharing grief in a stepfamily can be complicated. It's not as simple as I'm probably making it sound. It requires that you don't dismiss your spouse's, your children's, or your stepchildren's feelings. They need your support.

They need your permission to be sad. They need your grace on the hard days.

Sometimes all you can do is simply *be*. Galatians 6:2 tells us, "Bear one another's burdens, and so fulfill the law of Christ." A blended family has many burdens to bear, so take the time to find out what burdens the people in your home are bearing and do what you can to help them carry the load.

I'm not saying you have to weep with your current spouse over his or her previous spouse (awkward!), or urge your stepchildren to share their deepest, most sensitive feelings with you (ain't gonna happen!). They probably don't want you to even attempt that. Many people feel like grief is a private matter, so trying to literally weep *with* your blended-family members can easily come across wrong in so many ways.

But you can allow for sadness and respect their privacy. It's okay to get a little teary-eyed when they tell you a story about the person who's no longer around. Reassure them that it's totally normal and expected for them to miss the people they love.

Try to put yourself in their shoes. Remember how you felt when you went through times of deep suffering. Offer them the grace that God gave you.

Second Corinthians 1:4 says that "[God] comforts us in all our affliction, so that we may be able to comfort those who are in any affliction, with the comfort with which we ourselves are comforted by God." In other words, because God comforted us in our afflictions, we can now comfort others when they go through similar trials.

The goal in a blended family shouldn't be to make everyone comfortable and happy all the time. The goal should be to allow space and time for being sad some of the time so everyone can be happy most of the time.

A blended-family home should be a sanctuary for sadness. Even if everyone else in the world tells your family to suck it up and move on, in your home they should be able to remember and feel the sorrow of missing someone they love so much.

REMARRIAGE
AND WET FISH

I WAS TALKING TO A FELLOW CHURCH MEMBER about coordinating a special event for stepfamilies when a man overheard our conversation. He said, "Why do we have to have something special for *stepfamilies*? Why can't they just be *families*?"

"Wouldn't that be nice?" I said. "But stepfamilies don't work like first families." While I appreciated his desire to be inclusive toward stepfamilies, the reason stepfamilies have special events is that they have special *needs*.

Most family events or conferences tend to address issues specific to biological families, and stepfamilies often walk away still confused, saying, "They didn't address any of our problems!"

When the inherent differences between these two types of families aren't recognized, that's when the realities of blended-family life end up slapping unsuspecting remarried couples like a wet fish to the face. (Not every blended-family couple is made up of two people who are remarrying, but remarriage presents a special set of challenges, which we will deal with in this chapter.)

The Wet Fishes

Although rare in daily life, being slapped across the face by a wet fish is both painful and humiliating. Not to mention it leaves a lingering and unpleasant smell that offends everyone in your presence. It's just plain terrible all the way around.

It seems like there are countless issues just waiting to slap blended-family couples. Depending on your personality, situation, and spiritual condition, any number of them can take you by surprise and create chaos in your stepfamily home.

Let's start with issues specific to blended-family marriages. Marriage is the foundation of any family, including stepfamilies. A healthy stepfamily begins with a healthy marriage.

Most couples in a blended family share a bed, but they don't always share a life. Sure, they might discuss schedules and logistics, but in many cases, *she* takes care of herself and her kids while *he* takes care of himself and his kids.

That process might streamline various comings and

goings, but it doesn't focus on bringing the family—and especially the couple—together. When the kids are grown, that couple might feel like strangers.

There's a reason why so many remarriages struggle: Nourishing the relationship itself is often last on the to-do list. No one wants to be taken by surprise with a wet fish to the face, so let's look at some typical problems in hopes of being prepared when they arise. While I can't cover every potential pitfall in this book, I can highlight a few common issues for blended-family couples—many of which I've witnessed or experienced myself.

The Distraction of Dating

Grief is a lot like the blob from the old 1950s sci-fi film *The Blob*. At first, it seems more like a harmless nuisance that's easy enough to carry. But if allowed to grow, it starts to swallow up everything it touches. Eventually your whole life is swallowed up by unresolved grief.

Unresolved grief often shows up in the marriage because the remarried person didn't grieve properly during his or her single days. Some refused to cry. Others refused to talk about the death or divorce. Many use activities, habits, or work as distractions.

One popular distraction is especially tempting: dating. For men especially, searching for companionship often begins soon after the end of the first marriage. Dating is such a temptation because it's exciting. It feels good to think about the possibilities of new love, and it's thrilling to feel attractive, interesting, and wanted again. But mostly it is a distraction from the pain of loss, if only for a little while.

There is hardly a better feeling in the world than the tender touch of a warm hand after a lengthy period of cold, lonely nights. The endorphins are almost too good to pass up. So the lonely survivor starts dating way too soon, one thing leads to another, and before you know it, all those powerful emotions result in a marriage proposal.

When I first started dating again, a friend told me about a good Christian man she knew whose wife had recently died. It was just a few weeks into his widowerhood at the time, so I didn't want to introduce myself right away.

About six months later, I thought I should at least break the ice before some other woman jumped in. But it was too late. When I finally looked him up, he was already engaged!

Robbie certainly started dating too soon. He began looking for companionship within a few weeks of his wife's death. He had already been dating for two years when I met him, but even then, I knew he wasn't ready. I could tell that he still had grieving to do.

But I also knew Robbie wasn't going to slow down. So rather than pass him over—and lose him like the last guy!—I resolved to help him work through his grief as our relationship progressed.

In my case, I *officially* waited a year to start dating again. To me, that was an appropriate amount of time to respect David's memory. But behind the scenes, I had friends scouting guys for me within a month of my husband's passing.

Some might suggest that a person can grieve the loss of their first marriage while dating. But proper grieving requires actually feeling pain, working through tough questions, considering a new way of thinking, and forming a new identity.

Can all this be accomplished while at the same time enjoying the dating life? I'm not going to say no, since I imagine there are some who have dated and grieved at the same time successfully. But rarely do we humans willingly choose pain over pleasure. After all, dating starts the relationship ball rolling, and it's like a drug. Before you know it, you might find yourself married while still toting around a complete set of grief luggage.

The Spousal Burden

Another issue common in remarriages is the heavy burden on the new wife or husband to help their spouse work through the loss of the prior marriage. That process typically requires emotional, spiritual, and physical support.

Emotional support requires listening to memories and asking questions, plus sharing in the sadness or joy of those memories. Spiritual support involves prayer, a forgiving attitude toward outbursts of emotion, and patience as you work through it together. Physical support might require sorting through items left from the previous marriage. (This is typically less of a problem for remarriages that follow a divorce, as material possessions have likely already been divided.)

A spouse who remarries after a divorce will have to work through financial and child-support issues, custody schedules, and other legal paperwork. These sorts of issues can prove extremely difficult emotionally, which is why having the support of a new spouse is integral to building a strong bond in your remarriage. It's about becoming a team.

In the situation of remarriage after death, the new spouse might have to help go through items that belonged to the deceased spouse, since some bereaved people don't remove those belongings until they remarry. For example, when Robbie and I got married, he still had all Kari's personal possessions. Her clothes still hung in her closet. Papers and knickknacks were still in drawers and on shelves. Her jewelry was still in the dresser.

I asked Robbie's sons if they wanted to come look through everything, but they weren't interested. They told me to simply get rid of everything.

I knew better.

I reached out to Kari's mother, Becky, and asked her to come help us go through it all. If I had a question about anything, I talked to Becky and Robbie. Between the three of us, we sorted through everything and decided what should be done with it. It was probably good for Robbie and Becky to reminisce about what Kari's possessions represented.

Becky sometimes left the room, and when she returned, I could usually tell that she had been crying. I didn't mind at all, but I know she didn't want to make me uncomfortable.

Yet I did feel awkward going through her daughter's things. I thought it would have been better for her and Robbie to do it without me, but Robbie asked for my help.

So I tried to be very respectful and made sure they agreed before putting anything in the donation pile. I was probably more cautious than they were, because I knew there would be items that they'd later wish they had kept.

We asked the boys if they wanted any of Kari's personal items, like books or jewelry. They said no, but I kept them anyway. I kept anything that might have sentimental value, and I kept anything with her handwriting in it. I remember how sweet it was for me to find David's handwriting in a book or a letter.

There are several boxes in our attic that contain various items belonging to Kari, including a ceramic rabbit. Robbie would hide the rabbit in certain places around the house where he knew Kari would find it.

After each of the boys got married, they changed their minds about Kari's possessions. And they both expressed interest in some specific items.

In her book *I'm Grieving as Fast as I Can*, therapist and author Linda Feinberg explains the emotional importance of a deceased loved one's personal items. "If we possess something that someone we admire touched," Feinberg writes, "it makes us feel we have a little piece of him. The object becomes sacred."[1]

Even something as simple as a favorite mug can serve as a link to the past, and a new spouse must be careful to respect that. Robbie still has a set of matching Mickey and Minnie Mouse tumblers that he and Kari bought at Disney World. To this day, I won't drink out of either of them. I know it might sound silly, but to drink from "their" tumblers somehow feels disrespectful.

Genesis 2:18 says, "It is not good that the man should be alone; I will make him a helper fit for him." God knows we're not that good at dealing with life all alone. The burden is much easier to carry when someone is there with you, helping you along the way.

Jealousy of the Previous Spouse

When Robbie and I got married, I had a hard time finding a song to play at our wedding that expressed the love we had for each other. There were many popular love themes, of course, but many of them we couldn't say and really mean, such as *you're the best thing that ever happened to me*, or, of course, *you're the love of my life*.

I finally found a song titled, "The Second Time Around."[2] The lyrics express how a second love has its own special beauty, including the wisdom of experience and the softness of a deep appreciation for life. I'm thankful I found it, because there aren't many songs like that out there!

Having lost a spouse myself, I remember the feelings I experienced when it dawned on me that I would never be *the* love of Robbie's life. There would always be another woman who occupied a part of my husband's heart.

It reminded me of a scene in the movie *The Notebook*, in which the main character, Noah, had lost his true love. It seemed like Allie was gone forever. To assuage his pain, Noah dated a woman he didn't really love. The woman, however, loved him deeply despite his heart being elsewhere.

At one point, she cuddles up to him, desperately longing to see the love she can't have. She looks deep into his eyes and says, "A woman knows when a man looks into her eyes and sees someone else."[3]

There's an element of truth to that statement when it comes to a second marriage. It doesn't seem fair, but there are moments when that sentiment rings true.

Robbie and I can never truly say or hear the words "You're the only one I've ever loved." That reality can make me sad, no matter how much empathy I have. It can sometimes feel like the person you married loves you "second best," especially in the case of death or an unwanted divorce.

It can also create jealousy and fear if we let it. You might hear that ugly green monster whisper in your ear, *What if she someday wants to get back with him?* Or *Would he choose you or her?*

That's not a problem when the prior spouse is deceased, of course. The common issue with remarriages after a death is the near certainty of knowing that your new partner still loves the person who died, or—if you are the surviving spouse—wondering if you will ever be loved like you were before.

When dangerous thoughts like this come to mind, that's when I remind myself that Robbie is not my perfect husband. We are the bride of Christ, and no one loves us the way that Jesus does.

If you are remarried, you need to embrace the fact that your spouse can love you *and* the previous spouse. But it's not the same *kind* of love. After all, how can my husband love me in the same way he loved his high school sweetheart? The woman who bore his children? He can't. But he can still love me wholeheartedly.

I can't change the circumstances of our lives, but I can trust our God who uses all of them—including death and remarriage—for our good, just as Scripture tells us in Romans 8:28: "And we know that for those who love God all things work together for good, for those who are called according to his purpose."

I cling to the hope of knowing that it will all make sense on the other side of this life.

Comparing Previous Marriages

Remarried couples often fall prey to the trap of comparison. There are plenty of variations here, but let's look at two primary scenarios: the fabulous first marriage and the horrible first marriage.

With the *fabulous first marriage*, the surviving spouse regards the lost spouse as a saint of sorts. In his or her memories, at least, the first spouse was essentially perfect. The result is that nothing about the new marriage can ever measure up to the previous one.

It starts out with an innocent thought: *David would never have done this to me.* Or *Kari was never this picky.* But devoting too much time to these seemingly innocent thoughts can make us discontent with our current circumstances. A little comparison is normal, but this way of thinking can cause a person to doubt his or her choice of a new spouse.

When you dwell on all the ways that your current marriage is inferior, you tend to forget about the struggles in your prior relationship—struggles that often made you a closer couple.

We need to accept and to embrace the reality that no two people are alike; thus, no couple will be alike either. It's not always easy learning to live with a new spouse, with his or her nuances, habits, and quirks. But it's almost always worth the effort, and it usually enriches both of you along the way. Your marriage should be celebrated, not measured against a previous one.

Struggles are normal, especially early in the relationship. Sometimes it takes friction to make a relationship the best it can be. As Proverbs 27:17 says, "Iron sharpens iron, and one man sharpens another." Instead of focusing on how your relationship is not good enough, try thinking about how to make the marriage better.

Besides, if you somehow could marry someone just like your first spouse, would you really want to? How would you feel if your spouse said, "I married you because you reminded me of my first wife [or husband]"? (Um, no thanks!)

The second problematic comparison that can sabotage your relationship is the *horrible first marriage*. In this case, the prior marriage was not a healthy one and now one or both spouses want to do whatever it takes to create the perfect marriage. No matter the specific reasoning, they view the new marriage as "the chance to do things right this time."

This seems like a good idea, at least at first. But you eventually realize that there is no such thing as a perfect marriage. Even without the complications of blending two families, every marriage involves two imperfect people striving to become one.

As part of a blended family, you might have days where you feel like your stepfamily isn't happy with anything you do. If your goal is to have a perfect marriage, you will never be satisfied. Don't let that kind of thinking land you in divorce court. Recognize that the road to successful, blended-family life is a rocky one. Yet with God's help, you can make it to the right destination.

Will It Happen Again?

If you're a remarried spouse who lives with the fear of once again losing your partner, you are not alone.

In this scenario, the fearful individual puts up an emotional wall to keep from getting too attached to his or her new spouse. It's a defense mechanism of sorts—a type of post-traumatic stress disorder response, one designed to protect us from hurting that badly ever again.

Robbie had a hard time during the first few years of our marriage. He was still recovering from his feelings of sudden abandonment. I could tell that he wanted to be close to me, but the fear of losing another spouse to illness and death kept him from giving me his whole heart.

It plagued him so much that when we were in social settings, he would sometimes scan the room, looking at other women. When I confronted him about it, I discovered that Robbie had developed a habit of unconsciously looking for his next wife in case I passed away soon. This habit bothered me, but as we talked with other widowed men who've remarried, we learned that it's not at all uncommon.

I was disappointed to hear this, but I also understood his fear. Robbie certainly didn't want me to die, and we knew of no sickness that threatened my life. Then again, no one expected Kari to die either.

My new husband had to learn to trust God with my life and with his other relationships. And I had to learn to trust God that my new husband could love me *without* an insurance policy. It took a few years, plus a lot of prayer and communication, but eventually Robbie let his guard down and we were able to truly bond.

These feelings aren't limited to widowed people. Many spouses who were cheated on in a previous marriage often project those fears onto a new spouse. This can lead to someone who is always suspicious, always looking for clues that point to infidelity.

A sense of uneasiness is also common among spouses who were abused, except the person who was abused is constantly apologizing to the new spouse, taking on guilt that isn't warranted. In this situation, the other spouse might have a hard time getting the abused person to open up. Too often fear and mistrust will carry over from the previous marriage.

Grieving Alone

We humans are so emotionally complex that we can be happy and sad at the same time. That's why I can be perfectly happy with my current marriage *and* still miss my previous spouse.

Yet it's hard for many people to discern those simultaneous feelings in others. Most of the time we are perceived as being either happy *or* sad. Outward signs of grieving can create the impression that life for the griever is difficult.

This was one of the reasons why I felt so much pressure to grieve in silence. I was concerned that showing grief for David in public gave the unintended impression that I wasn't happy in my current marriage. I didn't want people to think I missed David because Robbie wasn't a good husband. He was—and is—a great husband!

For example, what if I posted something about missing David on social media? And what if it wasn't his birthday or the anniversary of his death? What if I just missed him? Then people might start to wonder, *Why does she miss David so much? Did Robbie upset her?*

Some remarried people also fear hurting their new spouse's feelings, especially if the spouse wasn't married before. It can be difficult to convince the person you recently married that lingering grief tied to the past isn't a reflection of the current relationship. That's why a sad, remarried spouse might try to hide those feelings from the current spouse. In turn, however, the current spouse may feel shut out and misunderstand the reason.

This dilemma can seem like a no-win situation: either openly admit your sad memories to your current spouse and risk hurting his or her feelings, or keep the grief secret, which can also result in hurt feelings.

So what should you do? It isn't always easy, but it's better to be honest with your new spouse and include him or her in your grief. The good news is that it will eventually bring you closer, even if it takes a while to get there.

You Are Not Alone

I hope the previous sections helped prepare you for some of the wet fish lurking in the shadows. And I hope you know you're not alone. The journey you're on can be difficult, but don't be discouraged. God is with you along this difficult path (see Matthew 28:20).

We remarried spouses are with you too.

With that in mind, I've compiled a list of guidelines I've learned along the way to help you navigate the potential pitfalls of blended-family life. These principles won't address every single issue you'll face, but they will help you work through your feelings and create a stronger bond with your spouse, no matter which one of you is dealing with a concern.

Let it go. Too many of us act like Elsa in the Disney movie *Frozen*—"Conceal, don't feel, don't let them know."[4] We live in a culture that wants us sad people to feel better.

But feelings need to be expressed. If you can't talk about

them with your spouse, try to find a compassionate pastor or counselor. Maybe you have a friend who can relate to the feelings you've experienced.

In our case, Robbie and I are blessed to have a pastor who understands our situation. His first wife passed away, and he got remarried to his college sweetheart. Of all the people Robbie has spoken with, he finds the most comfort in talking to this pastor. It's validating to know that another person has struggled with the same thoughts and feelings and understands that these thoughts and feelings are *normal*.

If you're the spouse who wants to help the other, do your best to be a good listener. Ask about the memories, feelings, and even the regrets. Let your spouse speak those experiences out loud. Laugh with your spouse and appreciate the chance to get a peek inside the deepest parts of his or her soul.

And if your spouse doesn't like to talk, don't try to force it. (I'm guilty of this sometimes, and it drives Robbie crazy.) The key is to let your spouse know that you are willing and ready to listen when the moment is right.

Yes, your spouse's emotions will likely involve memories of life with a previous spouse, but *you* are the one who is here right now. And one day *you* might be the spouse recalled in memories—the one who was there when you were needed the most.

Find your marital niche. God created both of you, so He is not surprised that you and your spouse are together now.

When Robbie and I go through a hard time, we often remind each other, "You are my precious gift from God." God knew there would be two deaths, and He knew that our relationship would form.

The same is true for your situation. Rest assured that God can equip you to be the partner that your spouse needs, and vice versa. Even if your spouse's prior marriage was filled with bliss, there are still aspects of your personality that can meet needs in your spouse's life that his or her previous spouse didn't.

It's like the way that a certain color shirt can bring out different colors in your eyes, or even seem to change the shade of your eyes completely. In the same fashion, you have the ability to bring out traits in your spouse that he or she may not have known were there.

Try to identify the unique contributions you bring to the relationship. (But please don't view it as a competition with the previous spouse.) Exploring new aspects of life with your spouse can feel a little like becoming a new person, especially if both of you were previously married. That may be an exciting proposition to some and scary to others. But don't let fear stop you. You might even have some fun!

For example . . .

Explore new hobbies and skills together. Robbie and I discovered several activities we enjoy together that our previous spouses did not. The first was our shared love of antique malls and flea markets.

Neither David nor Kari liked "old junk." But Robbie and

I enjoy the history of the items, the stories they tell, and the thrill of the hunt! In the same vein, we also love to tour old homes, such as historical mansions, plantations, and museums. Another activity we discovered was pottery. After a few years of marriage to Robbie, I noticed in him a flair for the arts. He had an eye for beauty and form, and I had a hunch that he would be great at art. We turned this hunch into an idea for a date night, and I was right! Robbie took to pottery like clay to a wheel. We both enjoyed it so much that we signed up for a ten-week class at the local art center. Robbie said he has never had more fun with me than taking that class together.

These new activities created a shared bond between us, and they give us fresh memories that aren't squeezed out by the old. They also allow us to expand our own interests and discover parts of ourselves that we didn't know were there.

Visit places where neither of you have been before. I love going back to the restaurant where Robbie and I had our first date and recounting the story of how he tried to hold my hand. It makes me feel giddy like I felt back then. There is something special about returning to a place of emotional significance.

The opposite is also true. If you visit places where your spouse shared special memories with a previous spouse, there will often be a sad sense of nostalgia. There's nothing wrong with visiting those places, but prepare yourself for the emotions that will likely arise.

You can't prevent the memories that come flooding back

at certain places. And sometimes it's good to reflect on the past. But family vacations or anniversary trips are not the ideal time to do that. So look for new places to visit and make fresh memories together.

Control your thoughts. This principle is for remarried spouses: Learn to control, as best you can, your thoughts about your previous marriage.

Your memories of the life you had with your previous spouse cannot and should not be forgotten, even if it was a difficult marriage. But it's important to consider exactly when you think about them and when you don't.

Author and theology professor Jerry Sittser wrote about the power of memories after he lost his wife, daughter, and mother in a car crash:

> Our memory of the past is not neutral. It can poison us or heal us, depending on how we remember it. . . . Loss can leave us with the memory of a wonderful story. It can function as a catalyst that pushes us in a new direction, like a closed road that forces us to turn around and find another way to our destination. Who knows what we will discover and see along the way?[5]

The Bible urges us to control our thoughts (see Romans 12:2; Philippians 4:8). That's because the thoughts we ruminate on have the power to influence our beliefs and actions.

Many remarried spouses let thoughts of their first marriage ruin their second marriage. Too many happy thoughts make you forget the hard days—the times when you didn't like each other very much. And too many bad thoughts can make you bitter and can even lead you to project past hurts onto your new spouse.

So rather than let your memories dominate your marriage, learn to control them. As soon as you think, *My first spouse wasn't like this*, remind yourself, *Yes, but that person's not here now. This is my spouse now, and this is the one who has my love, loyalty, and trust.*

You can't change the past, so you really have only two choices: Be happy with your new spouse . . . or not. Needless to say, the healthier choice is to be content with the spouse you have and learn to love him or her as they are.

Thank God for the spouse you have, and look for ways to grow together.

Make time for dating. I believe date nights are an essential tool for strengthening any marriage, but especially a remarriage that involves stepchildren.

In most first marriages, children come into the picture *after* the couple gets to know each other. Even couples who conceive on their wedding night have about nine months to build and enjoy their relationship without the demands of caring for children.

Couples in a blended family, however, rarely have the

luxury of time together without kids. That's why they need to *make* time. If you or your new spouse brought kids into your marriage, you need times when it's just the two of you—opportunities to strengthen your connection when the children aren't around.

It's also necessary to get away from the children at times because kids are often a source of stress in a remarriage. It's a virtual guarantee that there will be tension at some point between a stepchild and stepparent. And the biological parent often feels stuck in the middle.

There will be moments when a biological parent is tempted to take sides with his or her child, whether out of fear, a sense of loyalty, or even manipulation. That's when the stepparent can feel unsupported or abandoned. And that's not a good recipe for a healthy marriage.

If your time together consists mainly of coordinating schedules, dealing with money, working through issues, and other stressful and often unpleasant activities, then you definitely need time for just the two of you in an atmosphere that takes you out of "home mode." One of the best ways to do that is to schedule regular date nights.

Date nights let you get away, at least for a few hours, from the physical and emotional demands of parenting. Even better, date nights help remind both of you why you fell in love in the first place.

Robbie and I have a regular date night every Friday night, and I've learned that it's a very good thing. There were many

Friday nights when I did not want to go on a date with him because I was upset about something. But the sitter was coming, so I felt that I had to go.

One Friday evening I was having one of those *Why did I marry this guy?* moments. The house was in chaos. Everyone was raising their voices. You could almost hear the eyes rolling. But we departed on our scheduled date nonetheless.

When Robbie and I got to the restaurant, I sat across from him at the table, still reeling with emotion. I looked up and saw his shining green eyes looking at me lovingly. My expression softened. *There you are*, I thought. *There's the man I married. I missed you.*

Our time together was a breath of fresh air. By the end of the evening, I was reminded of what I loved about the man I married. It was just buried beneath all the emotional stuff that occupies so much of blended-family life.

Sure, it takes some work (and typically money) to find a babysitter, but I know of couples who swap babysitting duties each week. Or maybe a grandparent is generous enough to help give you a night out once or twice a month. No matter the obstacles, date nights are worth the effort. They are a wise investment in almost every marriage.

Prioritize your marriage. This is often difficult, at least at first, because as single parents we put everything into our children. We already love our kids so much, and then when a traumatic event like death or divorce takes place, it's easy to focus all our attention on the children.

Part of that focus is due to sympathy and sensitivity—trying to shield our children from any harmful issues caused by the trauma. And part of our focus is guilt. We're not sure if we've been the best parent, plus we're reacting to our own feelings of trauma.

When single parents remarry, we tend to keep making our children the top priority—focusing on their mood and their adjustment to blended-family life. We get caught up in the misguided belief that we have to make our kids happy in order to make up for the potentially traumatic event of getting remarried. We think that having happy kids makes for a happy home, so when we have to choose between our child or our spouse, we often choose the child.

Unfortunately, this is not the best approach at all.

Most kids enjoy the undivided attention they get from their single parent, and they don't want that to change. So when a new spouse enters the picture, that means competition for Mom or Dad. This was definitely the case for my little boy who was five when I married Robbie.

Yet part of the reason why Robbie and I married so quickly was for the sake of my young children. We figured that, at their young ages, Benjamin and Katherine would adjust better the sooner we stabilized the relationship. I thought my kids would soon be calling Robbie "Daddy" and accept him as the man in their lives.

But at five years old, my son had already become "the man in my life," and he started butting heads with Robbie almost immediately. Ben didn't understand why he couldn't sit in his favorite seat and have control of the television remote whenever he wanted. He didn't understand why this strange man suddenly had so much say in the rules of our house.

I was doing what my mother taught me to do, which is support my husband. But there was a big problem with that. Both my parents are my biological family members, and step-families don't function the same way as biological families.

Ben knew Robbie wasn't his "real" father. Moreover, at that point Robbie was still a virtual stranger! No other men had so much say in our house, not even uncles or grand-fathers. So why should this new guy be any different?

Robbie, meanwhile, wasn't used to this kind of pushback from his kids. Being a military man, he always taught his sons to respect his authority and respond with "Yes, sir" and "No, sir." Remember that Ben was just a toddler when his father died. He'd never had such an authority figure in his life before.

One day Ben was crying and complaining about how "mean" Robbie was to him, and I tried to explain to Ben that God set up a family to work this way. The father has a role of authority in the home, so he's someone whom we honor and respect. The mother, I explained, supports her husband and also has authority over the children, and the children need to honor and respect both parents.

My son looked at me and asked, "Do you love him more than you love me?"

It was incredibly hard to see his big, brown eyes fill up with tears, waiting for my answer. Ben knew I loved him.

What he really wanted to know was who had my loyalty. If I had to put one of them first, who would I choose?

This is where many blended families get it wrong. They think the best thing for the kids is to say, "I choose you, my child. Of course I love you more." However, even though it can feel counterintuitive for parents, the best way to love your child is usually to prioritize your relationship with your spouse. That doesn't mean loving your kids any less, and it certainly doesn't mean putting your children's best interests on the back burner (heaven forbid!). But it does mean that when allegiance struggles come into play, it's often best for everyone when spouses are on the same team.

I looked my young son in the eyes, knowing that he wouldn't understand if I said I loved Robbie more, so I said, "Are you still going to be living here when I'm old?" He wrinkled his brow, looking for an explanation, and said, "No."

"That's right," I said. "But Robbie will be. When you're all grown up, married to the woman of your dreams, working at your job, having kids, and living life, Robbie will be here with me. And you will be on your own."

If it hasn't happened already, your kids will put you in a position where you have to choose between them or your spouse. You won't be able to choose both. When that happens, choose your spouse. Not only because your spouse will hopefully be with you for the rest of your life, but also because it's the best thing for the children.

Kids need stability, and the only way to provide that is by building a strong family foundation—one that begins with a strong marriage. It's true that they won't like it. In fact, at times they will likely hate it, even if the family is otherwise healthy.

There are exceptions to choosing your spouse over your kids, of course—such as if a new stepparent is behaving in an abusive manner toward the children. I'll get into more detail about discipline within stepfamilies later on, including what to do when a stepparent is in the wrong. But the general principle remains: Try to side with your spouse whenever possible.

Grow together spiritually. Your marriage is the foundation of your home. You can't have a healthy home without a strong marriage, even in a blended family. And the strongest foundation is one built on the solid rock of faith in Jesus Christ and the Word of God. Jesus said,

> Everyone then who hears these words of mine and
> does them will be like a wise man who built his house
> on the rock. And the rain fell, and the floods came,
> and the winds blew and beat on that house, but it did
> not fall, because it had been founded on the rock. And
> everyone who hears these words of mine and does not
> do them will be like a foolish man who built his house
> on the sand. (Matthew 7:24-26)

How can we hear and obey Jesus' words if we don't know what Jesus said? Study the Bible together. Pray for each other.

Join an outreach team at church, host a small group, participate in missions.

If your foundation is strong, when you have done all you can and it feels like your household is falling to pieces, remember that Christ the Rock will never break or shatter. Families that are built on that Rock will survive the storm.

Learn as you go. Don't you sometimes wish God would use something other than trials to make us more like Him? Yet it's true that experience is often the best teacher. Many people will only learn the hard way!

So don't be discouraged. The struggles you go through as a couple are also lessons in patience, kindness, forgiveness, and other valued Christian qualities.

Every family is different, and you have no way of knowing when a wet fish will make an appearance and cause all kinds of problems. But you can be assured that God was not caught off guard, and He can use the most troubling circumstances for your good.

Just know that we're all still learning as we go. Only God has all the answers.

That's why, when you are frustrated and don't know what to do, go to God's Word. Read the Psalms. Read John. Read Philippians. And trust that even when you feel completely out of control, God is still in charge. He knows what's best for you and your family.

MYTHS AND FEARS IN BLENDED FAMILIES

IN CASE YOU HAVEN'T FIGURED IT OUT BY NOW, life doesn't always turn out the way we want it.

We like to pretend that we can control what happens. We think if we just live a healthy lifestyle, sickness won't intrude. Or if we follow all the "rules" of relationships, divorce won't be an option.

But we can't control our circumstances, no matter how good we are, no matter how many rules we follow. Bad things happen, and when someone you love leaves, either by choice or by death, it shatters the illusion of control.

When I first heard people describe grief as a journey, I thought they meant it happened step-by-step. And it does, in a way. But the journey of processing loss is more than just a physical or mental process. It's a deep dive into the soul.

It forces us to confront what we believe about the most existential questions in life: Is God really good? How can life be so fragile and terrifying? Why did this happen to me and not others?

While this personal battle rages on the inside, those on the outside have no idea. They go about their day. The hurting person, however, is left to wonder how life continues to move on for everyone else. For that person, life as they know it is over. And now they have to build a new normal from the ground up.

For a new blended family, this battle is happening for every member of the household. The adults aren't the only ones struggling. Each child involved also has to work his or her way through a tangled web of emotions.

As the parent or stepparent, it's important that you understand these emotions as much as you can. It's one of the ways you will help your family grow.

More than likely, you will have to help your spouse, kids, and stepkids work through their pain. They will need your understanding and grace as you all move through the next few years of blending the family.

That's why I put together lists of common myths and fears that affect blended families. Some were myths and fears that others had, and some were my own. Maybe you have some of them too. First, we begin with the myths.

Myth #1: Grief eventually ends.

As discussed before, grief doesn't simply go away. Instead, the individual simply learns how to live life a new way, like a person who loses a limb learns how to adapt.

My daughter, Katherine, was just three months old when her father died. Even though she now has a daddy she loves, I still grieve for those moments that David missed out on, like the time Robbie took her to her first daddy/daughter dance.

Of course, Katherine doesn't grieve those moments. She doesn't remember David at all, and I'm so thankful that she has a wonderful relationship with her stepfather. But *I'll* probably keep thinking about what might have been for her entire life. I'm sure I'll feel a wave of emotions when David isn't there to walk his daughter down the aisle on her wedding day.

Robbie feels the same way about Kari, even now that their kids are grown. Robbie wept for Kari at both of his sons' wedding ceremonies. They honored her memory during the services by having the bride place flowers where Kari would have been seated. Her absence was palpable.

It felt much the same on the day when the first grandchild arrived. Robbie was extremely happy and incredibly sad at the same time. Even though it had been years since Kari's passing, how could he not wish she were there to see the most beautiful little grandson in the world? That newborn was part of her legacy, yet she wasn't there to see his little face, touch his little fingers, and kiss his chubby little cheeks.

For stepfamilies after divorce, the loss is just as profound.

Not only does a child of divorce miss the absent parent, the child might wonder if he or she somehow caused the split. The child might experience bad dreams and long for the parent who is no longer in the home.

When a girl from a divorced family grows up, she might face choosing between her dad and stepdad to walk her down the aisle. Instead of simply enjoying the celebration, she might have to worry about hurting someone's feelings.

These losses and worries can last a lifetime. That's why demonstrating grace and mercy is so important in stepfamilies. Everyone needs the time and space necessary to work through the sadness that inevitably comes with a broken and blended home.

Myth #2: Everyone processes emotion the same way.

Because working through grief is often described as going through "stages," many people believe that grief is predictable and orderly. After all, the word *stages* implies that a person just needs to accomplish certain steps, at which point he or she will be cured or "over it."

Unfortunately, the word *stages* is a misnomer. Grief is neither predictable nor orderly. The five so-called stages of grief—denial, anger, bargaining, depression, and acceptance—are really more like phases that the bereaved can move in and out of. They don't necessarily happen in a certain order, and they can be repeated at any time.

For example, people can experience depression for several days, then feel hopeful and look forward to new changes, and then become upset for no obvious reason. They might bargain with God one day and be angry at Him the next. Eventually, they realize that they are starting to accept aspects of their new life, which might bring on more depression.

That's why it's a myth that everyone grieves the same. The five stages are recognizable for sure, but there's no certain way to tell which phase the grieving person will be in the next time you see him or her. And there's no way to predict or measure which stage people will go into next or how long they will be there. That's why a teenage stepchild can be friendly and even loving to a stepparent for months, then suddenly change and act like an enemy.

This emotional journey can be influenced by personalities, temperaments, and experiences, as well as by outside relationships, such as the relationship with a biological father or mother, siblings, or grandparents.

When several hurting people are all living in the same house, there is a complicated grief-network system going on at any given time. And it can be this way for years because no one is working through their grief at the same pace.

Whether adult or child, each individual will process grief differently. It's important to notice the signs of certain stages and find ways to let all the members of your family express their feelings in an understanding environment.

Myth #3: Toddlers and young children don't grieve.
This was a myth that I wholeheartedly believed. I thought if I could remarry quickly and get my children into a family with

a good father, they wouldn't be affected by grief. Nothing could be further from the truth.

Benjamin was two years old when David died. Katherine was a newborn. They don't have any memories of David, but they were still affected by grief in a number of ways.

First, they were affected by the grief of their mother (me). I tell people that when David died, I turned into an emotional zombie. When I wasn't crying my eyes out, I was lost in la-la land, reminiscing about the past and worrying about the future. Benjamin and Katherine saw me cry and get angry, cry and laugh, or cry and get irritated over the silliest problems. I could shift from tears to anger at any moment.

And because I was a stay-at-home mom, the kids and I spent almost all our time together. Even as toddlers, my children began to take on the role of emotional caretakers. Both of them learned to hug me and be sad with me. When Katherine was just two years old, she already knew how to say, "Mommy, it's gonna be okay."

To this day, if I show the smallest sign of sorrow—a crack in my voice, watery eyes, a slightly pink nose—they are immediately concerned.

"Mama, are you crying? What's wrong? Please tell me. What's wrong?"

Young children shouldn't be burdened with that kind of worry, yet my kids have been affected by my expressions of grief ever since David died. Even though they were both in diapers when it happened, their level of anxiety is still high today because of how it affected me.

Second, they have questions of their own when it comes to David's death. Many times throughout their childhood, my children have questioned how things might be different today if David had lived.

Robbie and Benjamin did not immediately get along, and they still have personality clashes on occasion. Ben sometimes wonders whether David would be a more understanding and patient father. And that, of course, is a question that none of us can answer.

The bigger issue, however, was that Ben went through several years when he blamed any and all of my sorrows on the fact that I was no longer married to David. (Since Robbie became "Daddy," my kids referred to their biological father as "David.") When our blended family first formed, there were naturally a lot of tears and hurt feelings. One day when Ben was particularly disturbed by my sorrow, he said, "If you were still married to David, you wouldn't be sad."

Ben had created an image in his mind that our family life with David was always happy, and our new life with Robbie was (in his mind) always sad. I had to explain to him that I was also sad sometimes when David was alive. Ben was surprised to learn that David occasionally hurt my feelings too.

It's vital that parents pay attention to the fears and worries of their children. After all, even many *adults* don't understand the emotional complexity and deceptive nature of grief, especially in a blended family. It's natural for children to see the unrest that comes with being part of a blended family and blame it on what they think is the seemingly obvious problem—the new parent.

This is a job for the child's biological parent. Only the biological parent can assure his or her children that the new stepparent is not the problem. The problem is the problem—blending a new family is hard and it's okay to be sad sometimes. God will work everything out in His time, even when it seems like things might never get better. Our children need to hear that they can trust God, even when they are sad.

Especially when they are sad.

Myth #4: A new parent will help fix things.

Some single parents believe that if they get a new spouse to take on the vacant role of mother or father in a child's life, then many of the child's problems will be resolved. Indeed, I've spoken with many stepmoms who married a man whose wife was either deceased or not part of her children's lives. And many of these women were heartbroken that the man's children wouldn't accept their mothering love.

This is a critical reality that stepfamilies need to recognize: No one else can replace a biological parent in a blended family. Especially if a child is old enough to remember the other parent, a new stepparent should *not* try to take over for the "missing" parent.

Consider how you might feel as an adult if your own mother or father died right now, and someone else—perhaps a virtual stranger—moved in and expected you to treat them the same way you treated your mother or father. Maybe that new person even pushed you to use the term *mother* or *father*. What's more, you're supposed to hug and kiss and offer your complete loyalty to this person.

Sounds ridiculous, doesn't it? Who would expect an adult to do that? So why do we expect children to push their parent aside, even if that parent is deceased, and embrace someone new with the same love and affection?

When I married Robbie, his son Seth was fourteen. I knew Seth was likely traumatized by the death of his mother when he was twelve. Knowing how important it was to me for my children to remember their biological dad, I worked hard to help Seth remember his mom. I wanted him to know that I respected his relationship with her and I wasn't trying to take her place.

A couple of years into our blended-family life, I asked Seth why he supported his father's decision to marry me.

Seth replied, "Because you didn't try to be my mom like the other women he dated."

It's important for stepparents to know that a child doesn't need a *replacement* for a parent, but they do need a male or female adult role model in their life. Perhaps as a mentor, and definitely as a supporter. In blended families that's the place for a stepparent.

Even if both of the child's biological parents are alive and well, all children need adult figures to serve as examples of a godly lifestyle. They need to know what to look for in a future spouse. They need both masculine and feminine perspectives on situations and decisions. A stepparent does have a role, but that role is *not* to replace the biological parent.

Myth #5: You can't be happy and sad at the same time.
As I mentioned earlier, our culture isn't comfortable with sadness. There are still stigmas around the idea of crying, such as these:

- It's seen as evidence of weakness.
- It "brings others down."
- It's a signal that something is wrong.

Maybe this negative view of sadness is based on the idea that if a person is sad, they can't be happy. But thankfully that's not true. Humans are complex creatures, able to experience conflicting emotions at the same time.

Many situations in blended-family life can create conflicting feelings, and often these feelings come up at very inconvenient times. I had an experience like that on the seventh anniversary of David's death.

The seventh anniversary was notable to me because I couldn't help but notice that he had been gone for seven years—the same number of years we were married. It became a kind of milestone for me.

As I was talking with the children about this upcoming anniversary, Katherine casually mentioned that she had never heard David's voice. That seemed incredible to me because

I had many video clips of David. That's when it occurred to me that I had never shown these videos to my kids.

I decided that I would invite David's family over to my house to honor David and watch the few brief videos I had. We all gathered around the television, and I eagerly anticipated my children's reactions. I thought they would be enthralled by the videos, curious to see and listen to this man they'd heard so much about.

When the videos played, we adults were overjoyed to see David. It had been so long since I'd heard his voice! But the kids only seemed interested for about the first five minutes. At that point they ran off to play with their cousins.

A little later, I heard Katherine behind me saying, "Daddy! Daddy!" But when I turned around to see her, she was calling out to Robbie, not David. She climbed up in Robbie's lap and watched the videos of her other daddy, David, on the screen, holding her as a newborn baby.

The moment was surreal. I was overjoyed that Katherine had a daddy in Robbie to take care of her and be the man in her life. I couldn't imagine my own life without my daddy.

At the same time, I was overwhelmingly sad that David wasn't here to enjoy his daughter's unconditional love. I remembered how proud he was to be a father, and how he was determined to be the best dad in the world—especially since his own father died when David was young and his mother never remarried.

I was both happy and sad at the very same time.

That's how life is for many blended families. Our feelings will toggle between the joy of God's blessings and the sadness of separation caused by death or divorce. Perhaps Solomon said it best: "For everything there is a season, and a time for every matter under heaven . . . a time to weep, and a time to laugh; a time to mourn, and a time to dance" (Ecclesiastes 3:1, 4). When we're feeling sad, we should let ourselves feel sad. And when we're happy, we should let ourselves be happy—even when we're feeling sad at the same time.

Such conflicting emotions can be particularly poignant during the holidays. I have certainly felt the sorrow associated with missing loved ones during the holidays. And I haven't felt it only for myself. I also miss Kari's presence for my husband's family.

Robbie's kids are old enough to remember Thanksgiving and Christmas with their mother. They remember her laughing and cracking jokes. They remember her special treats and quirky comments.

Those days are hardest for stepmoms, I believe, because "home" is more than just a place or a concept to mothers. It's also a sense of warmth and belonging. No matter how hard a stepmom works to make her home a welcoming retreat during the holiday season, there will always be an element of sorrow for the stepchildren. Home is never quite *home* without the people we love. (More on this in a later chapter.)

But we have to accept that it's okay to experience that element of sadness. Just because there's sorrow doesn't mean there can't also be love and joy.

Fears Associated with Loss and Grief

I've heard it said that Christian faith is not a vaccination against fear. Fear is a normal part of our humanity. This is especially true when it comes to trauma and loss. But through the Holy Spirit, we can move past those fears. We can't stop them from appearing, but we can stop them from controlling our lives.

Unchecked fear can slow the grieving process and keep people mired in depression. The following are some common fears I've discovered in dealing with grief. This list might help you identify some of your own fears and provide ideas for how to move past them.

Fear #1: We will forget the person who is gone.

After David died, I remember the panic I felt at the thought of one day forgetting him. Friends and loved ones told me I would be happy again and move on with my life. But that thought didn't comfort me. It actually frightened me. I knew David was someone worth remembering, and to "move on with my life and be happy again" only seemed possible if I could somehow forget him.

I learned later that I was mistaken, of course. I learned I could be happy and move on with life while still remembering my first husband. But that didn't stop me from crying the day I forgot how much David hated pickles.

I was talking to my sister-in-law about how Katherine loves pickles, and I playfully blamed her behavior on her side of the family. "Oh, no!" she replied. "David hated pickles! Remember?"

It had been years since David died, but it still crushed me that I'd forgotten something about him that I once knew so well. How many times did I order him a burger without pickles? Or hear him complain about people who seemed to put pickles in everything? I was devastated that I didn't remember.

Just the thought of "moving on" and no longer being sad can lead to feelings of guilt. Yet when children lose a parent to either death or separation, that's what we expect them to do. We ask them to call a new person "Mom" or "Dad," and we even expect them to have a good attitude about it. Maybe the possessions that belonged to their biological mother or father were removed when the other parent remarried. Some kids are even afraid of getting into trouble if they say, "I really want to keep that clock because it reminds me of my mom."

Even adult children struggle with these feelings of loss. Robbie's mother passed away from heart complications many years ago while he was deployed overseas. He didn't know when he kissed her good-bye that it would be the last time he would ever see her.

When Robbie returned a year later, he visited his father's house, expecting to grieve her passing. Instead, he discovered that the home was virtually empty of his mother's belongings.

To Robbie it felt like every trace of his mother had vanished. He wanted to connect with her in some way—eat at her kitchen table, sit in her favorite chair. But she had essentially been scrubbed away. He didn't understand how his father could move on so completely. Robbie wanted to ask, *How could you do this to me? How could you do this to my mom?*

Oftentimes parents are so anxious to start a new life that we leave the grieving kids lagging behind. We might be looking forward to moving beyond the old life, removing personal possessions, and finding love again, but the kids don't share those same feelings. What they feel instead is the fear that Mom or Dad will be forgotten.

Remember that it's not an either/or proposition. It's possible to move on and experience new happiness without forgetting the love and memories of the past.

Fear #2: Life is no longer stable or safe
for those who have experienced trauma.

I hope I've shown you that death or divorce and remarriage can be traumatic for all, but especially for children. Such life-altering events reveal a harsh truth about the world that most kids don't (and shouldn't) know until they are grown: Life is unpredictable and hard.

When the feelings of stability that a family provides are shattered, children often start to experience unreasonable fears. They might even revert to old fears they had when they were younger. For example, nightmares and panic attacks can surface. Bedwetting might become a problem.

While these issues should be dealt with for the child's sake, it's important that parents not scold or shame the child. This is a phase that will often resolve as the child works through the loss.

In the case of a death, many children worry that the same cause of death that took their parent might happen to them. I remember reading about a tennis star from the 1950s named Gem Gilbert, whose mother had died as a result of complications from a visit to the dentist. Gem was so scared of dying the same way that she vowed to never again visit a dentist.

Years later, however, she developed such acute tooth pain that her need for a dentist was unavoidable. Gem's pain reached the point that she eventually agreed to have a dentist come to her home. According to her obituary, she had both her doctor and her pastor by her side, but even they couldn't soothe her anxiety. Gem's fear was reportedly so overwhelming that she died at the mere sight of the dental instruments—before she even had any work done.[1]

Fear is a powerful emotion that can cause real damage to a person's mind. And children often don't understand the finality of death or even why it happens. In the book *Answering Your Kids' Toughest Questions*, authors Elyse Fitzpatrick and Jessica Thompson tell a story about one little boy who learned that his father had suffered a heart attack, fell out of bed, and died. The little boy didn't know what a heart attack was, so he assumed that his dad's death occurred because he fell out of the bed.

From that point on, the little boy was terrified to go to sleep for fear he might also fall out of bed and die. No one could understand why he was acting that way until someone took the time to talk to him about his father's death.[2]

Children, of course, aren't the only ones susceptible to a preoccupation with death. After David's passing, I became obsessed with the idea of death, to the point that I dealt with severe hypochondria and an anxiety disorder.

Plagued with worry about my two small children, I experienced multiple panic attacks a day. I thought I had symptoms of brain tumors, lung cancer, multiple sclerosis—I thought I had it all. I couldn't fall asleep at night because I wondered if I would still be alive the next morning.

My fears weren't limited to sickness or disease. Every time I drove across a bridge or through a busy intersection, my mind contemplated various steps of survival if my car, or someone else's, slid out of control. I constantly prepared for worst-case scenarios. I felt like the Grim Reaper was following me around, whispering in my ear all the possible threats to my life.

Eventually, I became overwhelmingly convinced that death is completely beyond my control. Sure, it's normal to struggle with the idea of death, but it's not normal or healthy to obsess over it. Based on my own experience, these struggles feel like torture. People who face these sorts of fears need help in overcoming them, so don't assume it's just a phase that will eventually go away. There are many therapies that can help one deal with anxiety, and medications prescribed by a professional can also serve as a bridge to a healthier mindset.

Fear #3: Some children blame themselves for their
parent's death or divorce.

It's vital to talk with children about a death or divorce because they oftentimes think that they might have caused it. The truth is that unless they are convinced otherwise, many kids come up with their own conclusions. And sometimes their reasoning defies logic.

Maybe a child said something mean to the parent before he or she died or left—perhaps something like "I hate you. I wish you weren't my mom!" Thus, the child wonders if God somehow took away that parent as a form of punishment for acting mean or angry.

Children might also think, *If only I had done this or that better, my mom/dad wouldn't have died or left.* Kids sometimes even blame themselves for not stopping their parent from going away, even in the instance of an accidental death.

In the case of a parent dying in a natural disaster like a flood or tornado, kids might suffer from survivor's guilt if they were rescued but the parent didn't make it. They might feel selfish if they were saved before the parent. And in cases of a life-ending disease, like cancer, some kids have blamed themselves for not making their parent eat better or live a healthier lifestyle.

When it comes to divorce, children might think that a parent left because they weren't well-enough behaved. They think that if they had acted better at home, Mom and Dad might still be together. A child might have even heard their parents arguing over parenting decisions and assumed that they were the main reason for the divorce.

Even though my kids were both babies when David died and they know he was killed in a car accident, they still get things wrong from time to time. At one point, the kids assumed that the accident was David's fault when it was actually caused by another driver. And not too long ago, Benjamin thought that David's extra weight might have had something to do with his death.

Kids pick up on different pieces of conversations, and their hardworking little minds can make connections that may or may not be reality. It's important, as they get older, to keep talking with your kids about a parent's death or reasons for divorce.

Most important, help them understand that God isn't punishing anyone by causing a loved one to die or to leave. Let them know that God isn't angry at them. In fact, God's character is full of compassion. Show them, as an example, how Jesus displayed compassion when Lazarus's loved ones mourned his death (see John 11:33-36).

Fear #4: Both adults and children worry that crying will make others sad.

Children, especially, think that their sadness might make everyone else sad. They might see their biological parent and stepparent happy together and assume that the grown-ups won't understand and might even be upset by their expressions of sorrow.

Kids often feel the same way about friends and peers. No one wants to be the downer in the group, so children often conclude that their friends won't understand their sadness—especially if the other kids' biological parents are still together.

Grief can be terribly lonely. A person overcome with sorrow often feels out of place because others generally can't relate to their overwhelmed feelings. It can seem like the grief will never end and that it's hard to imagine ever feeling happy again. Yet the very act of hiding our grief is one of the factors that can prolong it.

So make your home a safe place for showing emotions, especially tears. Let your kids know that crying is a healthy response to losing a parent, even if that loss occurred a long time ago. Reassure them that no one will be offended or upset by their sadness.

Kids also need to hear that the biological parent also misses Mom or Dad, even following a tough divorce. Even if you no longer want to be married to your ex-spouse, you can still assure your kids that you never wanted family life to turn out this way.

Try to find opportunities to empathize with your kids and lead them by example through those dark emotional tunnels. Let them know that there is nothing to be afraid of as you explore those feelings of sadness together.

God's Word and Communication

Myths and fears are powerful tools of Satan to confuse and discourage people. Our enemy wants nothing more than for God's people to be consumed with negative thoughts and feelings.

Here are two important Scriptures to keep in mind as you work through myths and fears common to blended families:

First, 2 Timothy 1:7 tells us that "God has not given us a spirit of fear" (NKJV). It is not God's plan that you should be overwhelmed with anxiety. God wants you to walk in faith, trusting Him to have all things under His sovereign control. Being free from fear means you are able to fulfill the purposes God has for your life and to experience the abundant life that He speaks of in John 10:10.

Second, 1 Corinthians 14:33 tells us that "God is not the author of confusion" (NKJV). God wants us to know the truth, and that includes the truth about blended-family life. It might be tempting to shelter or avoid some of the tough conversations, but that will only perpetuate more myths and misunderstandings.

In the end, talking about our emotions and working through various myths and fears can open doors to many spiritual conversations with your children and stepchildren. Use these opportunities to talk about the gospel and further understanding in your family.

It's really not that hard to talk to your children about these topics. Most of the time you just have to give them the freedom to ask questions.

I'm thankful for the person who noticed the fear inside the little boy whose dad fell out of the bed. Imagine how long he could have continued to live in unnecessary fear of his own death under similar circumstances! Thank goodness someone took the time to ask him about his fears and educate him about the truth. Thank goodness he can once again sleep soundly at night.

Make it a point to talk with your kids regularly about your blended family. Explain to them in age-appropriate terms what happened and what to expect. Their lives were changed dramatically by the end of your marriage—and again by your remarriage—so don't try to shelter them from the effects. Don't leave them on their own to hack their way through the jungle of anxiety and grief.

Fear makes people self-focused. Fear turns our thinking inward, concentrating on what we can do to save ourselves from the object of our fears. But when we discipline ourselves to think about others instead, fear usually dissipates.

If someone in your family struggles with fear, try to help him or her find a way to assist others. Maybe by volunteering with a local homeless shelter or other nonprofit organization. There are many Christian ministries, including your home church, that would probably love to have some help.

Most important, as you walk with your stepfamily through these emotional issues, remember to keep pointing everyone to the Word of God. Read Scripture and pray together as a family. There are dozens of Bible passages that speak about fear, hope, the purpose of suffering, and the character of God. Both you and your children will benefit from the hope and assurances found in God's Word.

THE INVISIBLE
FAMILY MEMBER

CLOSE RELATIONSHIPS can have a profound impact. If you're like me, you can point to many relationships—with parents, teachers, aunts and uncles, or close friends—that significantly influenced your life. Perhaps these people even changed the course of your future!

Of all our relationships, none (other than a relationship with God) will be more significant than the one with a spouse. Marriage makes two people so close that the Bible uses the word *know* as a euphemism for experiencing sexual intimacy. In other words, married couples don't just know each other; they *know* each other.

So just imagine the influence that a spouse has on your

life. Then again, maybe *influence* isn't a strong enough word. The marriage of a husband and wife is referred to in the Bible as "two becoming one" (see Genesis 2:24; Mark 10:8). That imagery reminds me of a pair of entwined trees located in a park just down the street from my house.

At first the two trees were young and they were close, but they were still separate. But as the trees matured, their root systems became entangled, drawing them ever closer together. Eventually the trees were so near to each other that the trunks morphed together, to the point that I can now no longer tell where one tree ends and the other begins. The two have become one.

The significance of a relationship that close doesn't suddenly disappear when one spouse dies or files for divorce. People are forever changed by that kind of closeness. You aren't the same person you used to be before you got married.

Children, of course, can't understand the significance of marriage when they are young. For a child, a parent is the closest relationship they can experience, and the importance of that parent-child relationship doesn't disappear or fade away after a death or divorce.

Some people assume that death or divorce in marriage is like a very bad breakup in a dating relationship. Sure, it might hurt for a while, but we eventually move on and rarely if ever speak or think about that person again.

Yet the end of a marriage is nothing like that, especially if the marriage lasted longer than a few weeks or months.

That's because after many years of marriage, two people

morph together, just like those trees near my house. Their lives become intertwined. They share wisdom and experiences. Their senses of humor become more in sync. Their arguments and discussions can change each other's behavior. Expectations are set. Routines are normalized.

For children, DNA plays a part. They are literally a product of both parents. There may be aspects of a child's personality that come from one parent or the other, whether it's a sense of humor, outlook on life, or self-image. Lessons learned from one or both parents make a lasting impression on a child's life.

And the longer you've known each other, the more profound the influence. Have you ever noticed that people who've been married for decades often display similar habits or expressions, like holding their mouths the same way or mirroring quirky behaviors and phrases? Some of these couples seem more like brother and sister than husband and wife.

In Robbie's case, twenty-two years of marriage to Kari wasn't enough to make them look like siblings, but they started out so young that they never really knew life without each other. They got married not long after graduating high school.

During those early adult years, a time when other people are discovering who they are and what they want to do, Robbie and Kari had each other to learn with. They were essentially still kids who learned their lessons side by side in the school of life.

Kari was there with Robbie when he joined the Army. Together, they moved overseas and experienced a new culture for the first time. When Robbie was deployed, it was Kari who kept things going at home. She was Robbie's stabilizer. Kari's picture helped keep him going on the toughest missions; she was the person he couldn't wait to come home to.

When Robbie retired after thirty-two years in the military, the Army honored him with a ceremony and all kinds of rewards. Unbeknownst to me, they also planned a special reward for Robbie's spouse in honor of the sacrifices made during his years of service.

I was honestly embarrassed to receive it. I didn't make very many sacrifices as a military wife. After all, we had been married only six years at the time. I never had to live through his deployments or pack up everything and move overseas. The most I had to endure was once-a-month drill operations, and even those took place on weekends.

I wanted to say, "Um, the wrong name is on this plaque. It should say Kari McDonald. She's the one who really deserves this award."

I think about everything those two went through together. They had each other's backs. They experienced the kinds of hard times that can either break or bond a marriage. Not only were their roots together deep, they were also strong. Kari is gone, but her influence is still a part of who Robbie is today.

These same things also apply to divorced couples. Even though divorce typically results from conflict, it can also be true that your spouse had a profound impact on you—for bad and for good. Unless you were married to a sociopath, there were almost certainly some good qualities about that person that you loved and admired, and maybe still do.

If nothing else, you had children together. And those kids are a daily reminder that something good came from your relationship. You can see your former spouse's face in those children. You can see similar character traits (hopefully good ones). And you can see how that parent—even if he or she is gone—will always have significant meaning for your kids.

That's why it's important to embrace what I call the "invisible family member" of your new, blended family. Unless you've made a conscious effort to erase all discussion of the past, you *are* going to hear stories about your spouse's previous spouse. The same goes for stories about your previous spouse. And that's okay! Laugh and cry along with the ones telling the stories. Listen and take it all in. Receive that information and store it in the files of your heart. Our memories are a big part of who we are today.

Many people struggle with this advice. After all, who wants to share a life and love with your spouse's previous spouse? Memories can stir up all kinds of difficult emotions, like jealousy and frustration, or feelings of inadequacy and comparison.

Yet if you want to know your current spouse inside and out, if you want to know your stepchildren, if you want to know *yourself*, then accept that the stories of your past include a very important person that can't be erased: a previous spouse. In the sections below, allow me to address some subjects that helped me understand and accept this truth.

The Ex-Spouse-in-Law

Those who have the most trouble with the idea of embracing the "invisible family member" are often the current spouses who have to deal with an ex-spouse. When it comes to divorce, ex-spouses are often portrayed as making life hard on the rest of the family. They might have a reputation for being jealous, mean-spirited, unreliable, or any number of annoying and destructive characteristics.

You may be thinking, *Why on earth would I want to embrace that person? And how could you ask me to do that? You don't know him or her!*

I understand. Perhaps he or she isn't a pleasant person. Maybe they heighten your own insecurities. Deep down you may be wondering, *What if he tries to take my new spouse away?* or, *What if I let my guard down and she sabotages our family?*

True, these scenarios are possible risks. They are small risks, but not completely implausible. Yet this person is also the biological parent to your stepchildren. This person has an important say in what happens in those children's lives. And no matter how much you might want him or her to go away, you are stuck with them for life. Yes, *for life*.

Even when the children living with you are grown, you'll still have to share any grandchildren with your ex-spouse. You'll likely see them at weddings, births, funerals, and maybe even holidays. Instead of hoping to live without them in the future, you're better off preparing to have them around.

Think of a former spouse like an in-law—or what blended-family expert Ron Deal calls the "ex-spouse-in-law."[1]

Just like an in-law, you don't have to be best friends with that person. You just need to be cordial and flexible. When you do that, the ex-spouse will feel the tension ease and maybe even let his or her guard down too.

If you can't do it for yourself, do it for the kids. Your stepchildren will notice when you make an effort to reach across the aisle. If the ex-spouse doesn't return the favor, the kids will likely see that, too. Kids often struggle to adjust to traumatic situations, but they are usually aware enough to notice what's going on around them.

Cordial co-parenting will go a long way in the eyes of your stepchildren. And it's the kind of emotional investment that can really pay off when the kids are grown.

There's Enough Love for Two

Another group that might struggle with embracing the previous spouse is the current spouse of a widowed person. It's hard to deal with the fact that your spouse loves another, even if that individual is deceased.

We have to remember that our hearts are big enough to love many people at the same time.

I remember when I was pregnant with my second child. I looked at my firstborn toddler and wondered how I could ever love another baby as much as I loved him. That thought worried me, so I asked my mother how she did it.

"Sabrina," she said, "there is no limit to how much you can love. There is enough room in your heart to love more than one baby."

As soon as I saw the newborn face of my big-eyed, chubby-cheeked daughter, I knew my mom was right. My love for my children filled every nook and cranny of my heart. My kids are different in almost every way, but I couldn't love either of them more than I already do.

I faced a similar fear when I married the second time. How would I be able to love another husband as much as I loved David? But my mother's words came back to me, and they still ring true today—there is no limit to love. There is enough room in my heart to love both husbands. Despite their differences, I love each one as much as the other.

Of course, I don't love my two husbands exactly the same way. No one could make me laugh like David did. Our personalities had so much in common, we used to joke that we must have been separated at birth.

And when I was a tender young woman, creating my place in the world, David was there, facing the unknown with me. He was my first love and the father of my children.

Robbie, meanwhile, brings a whole new level of depth to my life. He is brave, adventurous, and there's nothing he can't do! He has the outdoor skills of Davy Crockett and the lion heart of King Richard. He can kill a deer, skin it, and cook it up for dinner; and in the same twenty-four-hour period, he can take me dancing downtown and come home singing the tunes.

I don't have to choose who I love most. I love them both with all my heart.

But David is gone. Robbie is my husband now. So I give Robbie my respect, help, attention, and the focus of my love. David no longer has need of me as a wife. Robbie is my priority because he is the one my heart belongs to until one of us dies.

It's much the same with Robbie and Kari. He could never love me the same way he loves her. I'm not the mother of his children. I wasn't supporting him when he was fighting for his country in Iraq. But now I am the one who cares for him when he's sick; I'm the friend when he's lonely. And I'm the one who'll be with him during the different trials we'll face in the second half of life.

If you are married to someone who was widowed, I'm confident that your spouse loves you for you. You aren't loved more or less than the previous spouse. Just like we parents adore all our children, there is plenty of room in a spouse's heart to love more than one person.

No Marriage in Heaven

If you're remarried, have you ever wondered to whom you will be married in heaven? Will it be your first spouse or your second spouse? And what if your first spouse *isn't* there? Will God still let you be married to your second spouse?

The Sadducees once asked Jesus a similar question

(Matthew 22:22-33). They described a woman who had seven different husbands, all brothers, one after the other. They wanted to know which brother would be the woman's husband at the resurrection. Jesus replied, "In the resurrection they neither marry nor are given in marriage, but are like angels in heaven" (Matthew 22:30).

When Jesus said we would be like the angels, He didn't mean we would all wear white robes and grow wings. He meant, just like angels, we wouldn't have spouses or participate in any kind of marital activities. There will be no need for the institution of marriage.

Marriage serves two important purposes on earth. First, it is the nucleus of the family. God's plan for the family is for a man and wife to create children and to raise those children. That was the first instruction given to Adam and Eve in the Garden of Eden. God told them to "be fruitful and multiply and fill the earth" (Genesis 1:28).

Second, marriage serves as a reflection, a model, of God's great love for His people. The apostle Paul explained this in Ephesians 5:31-32 when he wrote, "'Therefore a man shall leave his father and mother and hold fast to his wife, and the two shall become one flesh.' This mystery is profound, and I am saying that it refers to Christ and the church."

There is a reason why Jesus refers to Himself as the "Bridegroom" (see Matthew 25:1-12; Mark 2:18-22; John 1:28-30). He uses this terminology because marriage is the relationship on earth that comes closest to reflecting the way God loves us.

It's not an exact reflection, of course, but it does parallel the way God has made a covenant with His people. In heaven, we will finally enjoy the ultimate fulfillment of our covenant with Christ, as His bride, and there will be no more need for a marital covenant between man and wife.

Yet some Christians have a mistaken view of earthly marriage in relation to this topic. Some widows and widowers avoid remarriage because they think it's like cheating on their deceased spouse. I once spoke on the topic of remarriage at a retreat for widows, and a woman approached me afterward to tell me about a widowed friend of hers at work.

Her friend and a single man had become close, and the woman hoped they might have a relationship. But the man said it was impossible for him to marry again, even though his wife was dead. When the woman asked why, he told her it was because he knew that when he died, he would still be married to his wife in heaven. To him, marrying another woman felt like cheating.

Until this woman heard me speak, she had never heard Jesus' words from Matthew 22. She was so happy to have Scripture to show to her friend.

There is a reason the wedding vows say "till death do us part." When one spouse dies, the covenant with that person has been fulfilled. It wasn't broken or put on hold. If your spouse dies, your promise was kept and fulfilled, and you are now free to create a new covenant if you desire to do so.

Clash of Cultures

The marital relationship you once had with your first spouse might be over, either by death or divorce, but the lingering effects of your relationship with that person are still very much intact. And that relationship's influence on your new marriage is also very real.

As I said earlier, your previous spouse had a role in making you who you are today. Getting married again involves a sifting process—retaining certain aspects of yourself from that prior relationship and moving on from others. Both partners are essentially combining several different aspects from their pasts into this new family.

Think of it this way: A first marriage is like moving to a foreign country, let's say Spain. It takes time to learn the Spanish language, customs, traditions, holidays, cooking, everything. You learn to accept new ways of doing things, even though they may be completely foreign to you. But just when you start to get acclimated, your house burns down, you lose your job, and you're forced to pack up and move to Germany.

Very little of what you learned in Spain is going to help you in Germany! The language is different. The traditions and customs are different. The food is different.

In the same way, a first marriage—even if it was a healthy one—prepares you very little for the second. It's only good preparation if it taught you to be flexible, because almost nothing will be the same as it was before.

Every marriage has its own characteristics. There are

certain foods, prepared a certain way, that everyone loves and looks forward to. There are certain words that convey added connotations, both good and bad. Every couple has a distinct communication style—some are loud and boisterous; others are quiet and reserved. Yet everything changes with a blended family, and there are all kinds of unwritten rules that the new family members will have to work their way through.

This is one of the many reasons why it's helpful to understand the previous spouse. You shouldn't try to mimic that person or try to replace someone, but it's helpful to understand them because that knowledge can assist you in better relating to your new spouse and stepchildren. You don't need to walk in the prior spouse's shoes, so to speak, but a partial education is better than none at all.

Consider love languages, for example. You may have heard of Gary Chapman's well-known book, *The 5 Love Languages*. Chapman developed categories for the ways that people like to give and receive love. Chapman's theory is that virtually every act of love can fit into one of five categories: words of affirmation, acts of service, gifts, quality time, or physical touch.[2] Some people use multiple expressions, of course, but every person has a *preferred* method for expressing and receiving love.

Therein lies a problem with second marriages: The way a remarried person learned to express love to a prior spouse likely won't be the same in a new relationship. In other words, both of you will probably need to learn to express love in a new way. And this education will take time and a whole lot of trial and error.

This was a big problem for Robbie and me early on. His first wife's preferred love language was acts of service. Kari didn't crave physical touch, but I'm all about cuddling, holding hands, sitting close—all the touchy-feely stuff.

When Robbie and I got married, he behaved as if my love language was also acts of service. He would happily do dishes, laundry, or tinker with some broken appliance. I, meanwhile, wondered if he was finding ways to avoid me. So I chased him around the house, trying to wrap my arms around him or luring him to sit next to me. I couldn't figure out why Robbie was so standoffish.

My first husband, on the other hand, loved to be rubbed and to have his back scratched, so that's how I learned to express love. I sat down next to Robbie in the evenings and scratched his back or rubbed his shoulders. When he would recoil or grunt or move my hands away, it left me feeling totally rejected. I couldn't understand why he refused my demonstrations of love.

It turns out that Robbie felt smothered. He couldn't understand why I seemed so needy.

And if that's not confusing enough, love languages can also *change* in a new marriage. In Robbie's marriage to Kari, his primary love language was physical touch. Robbie needed physical touch from Kari because he received a lot of love from her in other ways.

Yet with me, he often gets an overabundance of physical affection. So now his primary love language is quality time.

Robbie always wants me to join him on his adventures, even if it's just a trip to the hardware store.

It took us a long time to figure out each other's primary love language. It also took a lot of understanding about how we interacted with our previous spouses.

A person who remarries after a divorce might tell stories of how his or her love language was never spoken by a previous spouse. This information is also helpful because it can reveal what *not* to do.

Thankfully, Gary Chapman and Ron Deal teamed up to write a book specifically for people like us. It's called *Building Love Together in Blended Families: The 5 Love Languages and Becoming Stepfamily Smart*.[3] I recommend that all remarried couples read it, no matter the circumstances of your previous relationship. It can help you work through the confusion of how to demonstrate love in ways you probably never considered in the past.

Love languages are just one of the many cultural hurdles that come with building a new relationship. It usually takes a lot of time, patience, learning from mistakes, and even more time to figure it out. And even when you achieve somewhat of an understanding, it's still hard to keep moving forward.

But do it anyway. If there is one thing I've learned in our blended family, it's that none of us are perfect. None of us have all the answers. And all of us have baggage from the past. So don't be afraid to rummage around in that baggage and dig up what's been holding you back.

My Way or the Highway

"I thought everyone did it that way!"

Have you ever heard someone speak those words, often with a tone of disbelief? I'll never forget my first Christmas married to David. His family tradition was to have zero presents under the tree until Christmas morning. That's when stacks of presents appeared overnight, and every single gift was from Santa Claus.

David thought of that as a magical childhood experience. To go from nothing to everything overnight was the crowning moment of Christmas for his sister and him.

I, however, was appalled when David described his family tradition. In my home growing up, we had presents under the tree during the whole holiday season because we all gave gifts to each other. We gazed excitedly at the packages, wondering what was in each one. Only one big gift on Christmas morning came from Santa.

The exchanging of gifts between members of the family was one of my favorite parts about Christmas. I loved getting a music box from my father or a long-awaited doll from my mother. It made those gifts extra special coming from a person I knew and loved.

That's why it was so strange for me to consider the possibility of changing that tradition. *I thought everyone did it our way!* It never even occurred to me that a modification of my childhood Christmas routine would be a part of getting married.

Not a big deal, right? Well, these are the sort of small

differences that can become big issues in a blended family. A Christmas compromise like the one David and I negotiated only affected the two of us. No kids were involved yet.

But in a blended family, both parents and children (and in blended families, that might mean *several* children) are impacted by these differences. Kids who were raised to celebrate holidays a certain way can come to believe that way is the correct and only way. If a stepparent does things differently than the biological parents, then in the children's minds the new way is wrong. And not simply wrong, but sometimes *egregiously* wrong! In reality, kids don't really want you to be *like* their biological parent. They just think all *good* parents can do the things they are used to. Therefore, in their way of thinking, if you can't do it, you aren't good.

Traditions and met expectations make life feel stable for us humans, especially kids. Our customary practices help us feel secure and comforted. Thus, when something interrupts or disturbs those practices, we often feel unstable. We start to wonder what other things might change and if the people and traditions we've grown to treasure will ever be the same.

That's one of the reasons why it's hard for children to bond with a stepparent. The stepparent will understandably do many things differently—not bad or wrong, just different—and that leads to feelings of instability. It can bring up all sorts of questions and fears.

As I mentioned earlier, biological parents play a significant part in shaping their kids' identities. A parent's habits, stories, dreams, attitude, and humor are all filtered through a child's senses and will influence (for good and for bad) the child's personality.

When a biological parent is no longer around—or no longer around as much—those aspects of the child's personality don't simply disappear. The closeness to that parent lives on through the common bonds of ritual and tradition. So for a stepparent to change the way those things are done, or even take them away, is to cut off another connection to the missing parent.

I'll address specifics about the changing nature of traditions later in this book. But for now, I'll point out that a child's connection to his or her parents goes far beyond holidays or family gatherings. For example, an older daughter will often take on the "mother" role after a death or divorce. She might get used to making decisions about meals or helping younger siblings get ready for school. The daughter might see this role as her new duty—a way to make her biological mother proud.

But when a stepmother joins the family, she might view this role as a "burden" on her stepdaughter. With the best of intentions, the stepmother might relieve her new stepdaughter of these duties so that she can be a kid again, like all the other children her age.

The stepdaughter, meanwhile, might feel that her stepmother is taking away her important contributions to the family—and, even worse, is taking away her connection to her biological mom.

It's true that existing tensions in the relationship might

make it awkward to have these difficult conversations, but the wrong way to handle the situation is to never talk about it. Left unaddressed, misunderstandings about traditions and expectations can ruin the happiness of a blended family.

"David Never Would Have Done That."

In addition to holding on to certain ways of doing things, many kids tend to forget all the unflattering things about the parent who's no longer around. Losing someone close has a way of altering our perspective. So annoying habits, arguments, and imperfections now seem minor compared to no longer having that person in our life.

This tendency to see only the good seems like a wonderful quality. Our brains have the ability to suppress bad memories and hold on to the good. But that can be a hurdle when it comes to adjusting to life with a stepparent. There's no way a stepparent can compete with idealized memories of a biological parent. Sometimes the kids can't remember anything negative about the biological parent, while at the same time, they have a hard time seeing anything positive about you.

Even my biological kids, who didn't really know their biological dad, will sometimes say, "David never would have done that." They say it so emphatically, as if they know! But they have no idea. They've created a made-up picture of who they think David was, yet that picture is all about what a wonderful person he was and never about any of his flaws.

As the stepparent in this case, you can only keep reminding

your stepchildren (and yourself) that you are not perfect. You are going to make mistakes. And when it's appropriate, admit your mistakes and ask the children to forgive you.

Another issue that keeps children from noting anything bad about a biological parent is their built-in loyalty. Some kids feel that to say something negative about an absent parent is a sign of disrespect. This loyalty issue is also why some kids struggle to accept a stepparent even when the biological parent is dead. They think the deceased parent's feelings would be hurt somehow if they knew that the "replacement parent" was accepted and liked.

These reasons and more are why your stepchildren need your grace and understanding when it comes to the parent they lost. Help your stepchildren realize that you are not a replacement, nor are you an enemy to their mother or father. You view yourself as an addition to the family, and it's fine for them to see you that way too.

You're Not the Biological Parent, and That's Okay

A stepparent is just that—a stepparent. You can't replace a biological mother or father, especially when that parent is still around or when the child still has memories of that parent.

When I married Robbie, his son Seth was grateful I didn't try to *be* his mother. I put myself in a position of authority, like a teacher or a boss, but I never presumed to be his mom. He already had a mother, and I wasn't her. I was a new person in his life, and both of us were okay with that.

In the case of my own children, *I* was the one who feared that David would be replaced. I wanted everyone, especially his kids, to remember him—his personality, talents, humor, and all the contributions he made.

But I now realize that David will never be completely forgotten. People leave an impression on the heart and soul of everyone who knew them and played a part in their lives.

Yes, someone else married David's wife and helped raise David's kids, but Robbie isn't David. And there are still days when I think, *I wish David were here,* because there is no one else who could meet a particular need like he could.

Your stepchildren need to know that you recognize the valuable influence of their biological parent, even if they don't remember their mom or dad, like my kids don't.

It's not as hard as you might think. You might remark how you can see their mother in the way they smile. You can suggest that their great sense of humor must have come from their father. Or you can simply say, "I know your mom/dad would be so proud of you."

When you diminish your spouse's first wife or husband, however, you are in essence saying to your stepchildren, "I don't like who you are." No amount of embracing the children will make up for that perceived rejection.

A blended-family home should be a place where all the family members can celebrate the people they love and not feel ashamed. If you force them to choose loyalties, they will. And you probably won't be their first choice.

A Place of Honor

When I say you need to accept a previous spouse, I want to be careful here. Many stepparents want so badly to be an integral part of a stepchild's life that they overstep their bounds. This is especially true in families where the first spouse is deceased.

You don't want to act more concerned about the previous spouse than your new spouse or your stepchildren. This almost always comes across as insensitive or intrusive.

If the members of your family don't want to celebrate the deceased person's birthday, then don't force it. If they aren't interested in commemorating the anniversary of that person's death, then don't create one. If they choose to do something special, then go with it. But be supportive, not pushy.

Perhaps you want to help honor the deceased person in some way, and that's fine. Just don't overdo it. Maybe it's as simple as watching a family-favorite movie on a special anniversary, or displaying a treasured photo of the entire family. That doesn't mean you have to keep a portrait from your spouse's previous wedding on the mantle, but it doesn't hurt to have a photo in a place where the children can see it. This is a way of showing that you support their memories of the deceased and that you have accepted the person as part of your family.

Early in our marriage, I noticed that Robbie had lots of family videos, but they were all on videocassettes. No one in his family could watch them because VHS players had already become obsolete.

So one Christmas I had all their home videos transferred to DVDs and gave them as gifts to my stepsons. Robbie's oldest son, Will, told me how much he appreciated the gift, even years later.

There is also a wall in our home with pictures of David and Kari and some beloved family photos. It's alongside a staircase that's visible from the living room, so the kids can see the pictures on the way to their bedrooms.

Once again, I caution new stepparents to avoid going too far. Stepparents are typically seen as outsiders to the children's "real" family, so if you make a big deal out of honoring the parent who is no longer around, it can be seen as insensitive or intruding. It's a mistake that can cost you relationship points, even when it's done with the best of intentions.

"You're Not My Mom!"

Even though I encourage embracing the memory of a prior spouse, I know that can be hard for many stepparents, particularly stepmoms. Because women in general have a stronger maternal instinct, it can be hard to understand that while bereaved kids need a caretaker, they don't need another mother.

Mom is a special role that's already been filled, but stepchildren can still love you, albeit in a different way—perhaps like a favorite aunt, coach, or mentor. Don't build a wall just because you can't replace their biological mother. Carve out your own niche in their lives.

Your relationship can also change as your stepchildren get older. If they are still young when you married their parent, they may feel as close as your own children, only to become much more distant as teenagers. They might start saying things like "You're not my mom!" But those same kids often mature and realize that it's okay to be close after all.

If you can embrace the changing nature of your relationship right from the start, it will be much easier for you to remain flexible as stepchildren grow and change.

Stepchildren might never love you the same way they loved (or love) their mother, but that doesn't mean they don't love you at all. They just love you differently. It's like when I discovered that a parent can love more than one child. You don't love one more than the others, but you do love them differently.

Step-In-Laws, Your Best Allies

When a single parent remarries, the whole family is impacted. We don't often think about grandparents and in-laws, but a remarriage can be a scary time for them as well. They already have a lot of love invested in the family and they don't know how things will change with a new spouse involved in raising the kids.

Doubts and fears are rolling around in their heads. *Will they be accepted by the new spouse? Will they still get to see their grandkids? Will they have any influence in the family?*

The grandparenting years are supposed to be a time for passing on the family legacy and enjoying the fruits of marriage and child-raising. But in the case of a remarriage, at least one set of grandparents no longer has a child in the home to ensure that a relationship with their grandchildren will continue.

When Robbie and I married, we each came with a set of in-laws from our first marriage. We refer to these family members as "step-in-laws" when we're talking to others about our blended-family situation.

I already told you the story of how David's mother, Joy, accepted Robbie, but let me tell you how I got to know Robbie's in-laws.

Robbie was like a son to Kari's parents. Ray and Becky knew Robbie when he was a teenager dating their only daughter, so they literally watched him grow up. And when Kari got sick, they moved three hours from their hometown to help care for Kari, as well as Seth and Will, their only grandchildren.

After Kari died, Ray and Becky remained in town to help Robbie with his boys. They attended church together and ate lunch as a family every Sunday. They were a close-knit bunch.

When Robbie and I married, he moved to my town about thirty minutes away, but we decided to stay at the church his family attended. That meant I was going to be sitting in the same row as Robbie's in-laws and eating lunch with them every Sunday.

I had no idea how Ray and Becky would respond to me. Would they direct any unresolved grief toward me? Would they reflexively side with their grandsons if I did something they didn't like? I had no way of knowing what kind of relationship awaited me.

I could tell that Ray and Becky were just as apprehensive of me at first. They had no idea what kind of person I would be. Would I welcome their input? Would I be jealous of Kari's memory? Would I treat their grandsons with kindness?

As the weeks went on, we got to know each other better. They became like family to me. It was as if we had always known each other.

I will never forget the day Ray hugged me as we were leaving after lunch. "You're our daughter now," he told me. "No matter what. You're one of us, and I love you."

From that day forward, he has never left my company without telling me he loves me.

For a father to say that to his son-in-law's new wife—there's no other way to explain it than the influence and presence of the Holy Spirit. Both Ray and Becky loved me with a supernatural love, the kind of love that Christians have for one another.

And that same love carried over to my two kids. They basically became another set of grandparents to Benjamin and Katherine. The kids started calling them "Pop" and "Meme Beck" almost from the start.

One day Becky asked me, "Is it okay if I call Ben and Katherine my grandchildren? I just wanted to make sure it was okay with you." I was elated! I was so happy that she loved my kids that much.

"Pop" and "Meme Beck" come to every birthday party, plus Christmas, Thanksgiving, and every other holiday when the family gathers. I couldn't love them more if they were my actual flesh and blood. (It took my kids a few years to understand that Ray and Becky weren't their biological grandparents, but they were the real deal as far as I was concerned.)

Becky became a mentor and friend to me. When I had trouble knowing how to relate to Robbie's kids (and even Robbie!), she was a listening ear and a source of wisdom. And most important, she was like a bridge for the entire family.

When a mother dies, the grandmother often fills her role as the matriarch of the family. This was certainly true in Becky's case. Since both Robbie's mother and Kari had untimely deaths, Becky was the only female relative left in the immediate family.

That position gave Becky a certain amount of influence that I didn't have. If I knew a touchy subject needed to be addressed, I would talk to Becky. She would either advise me how to handle the subject or speak on my behalf.

Sadly, Becky died just five years into my marriage with Robbie. I have felt her loss nearly every day since then.

I realize that not everyone has step-in-laws as gracious as mine. If you have a positive relationship with your step-in-laws, count your blessings and don't overlook what they might have to offer.

After all, they have history with your family that you don't have. They understand the importance of certain places and objects that you don't understand. They can help you piece together information to give you better insight into the people you now live with.

So gather all the wisdom from their hearts and minds that you can.

On the other hand, some step-in-laws will still be grieving the loss of their adult child even many years later. Some might even take out their anger or sorrow on the new spouse. As hard as it is, try to have empathy for their great loss and pray that their hearts are softened. Turn the other cheek. There might be times when you need to confront their behavior, but try to seek peace whenever possible.

Now, if it's *your* parents who are causing problems for your new spouse, don't let it go. Talk to them. Remind them that you are loyal to your new spouse and that you expect them to treat that spouse with love and respect.

A Fuller Picture

Getting to know your spouse's previous spouse is a daunting task. And it's virtually impossible in the case of death. You can't truly know someone who died any more than you can know an ancestor. You can hear about them, look at pictures, even watch videos—but that's not the same as really *knowing* someone.

Besides, people are much more than just pictures or stories. Life is all about presence. There is something about the way a person carries herself, the way she moves, the way she speaks and responds to others. You can't get any of that from photos.

It's almost as difficult to get to know an ex-spouse who's still around. There is often tension, jealousy, and mistrust, especially if there is a history of hard feelings. You might not be able to talk to the person privately or even directly.

But you can still learn some things through the way your family talks about the person. You'll start to see what's important to the ex-spouse and what aspects of the previous family life influenced him or her the most. You might see some faces light up, or countenances drop, depending on the particular memory or story.

The more you can learn about the person who preceded you in the family, the more you will learn about your blended family as a whole—and the more your family will trust you with their memories, even if they are painful. You can never fully replace that person, but you can become a listening ear, a confidant, a friend. And isn't that what we all really need in our family?

A DIFFERENT KIND OF PARENTING

I DON'T KNOW ANYONE who said as a little girl, "I want to grow up to be an evil stepmother." Yet here I am. Nailing it! Thanks to Grimms' fairy tales and Hollywood stereotypes, stepparents automatically start off in a negative light, especially stepmoms.

In *I'm Grieving as Fast as I Can*, Linda Feinberg tells the story of an eight-year-old girl who was very attached to her widowered father's girlfriend.[1] The girl loved the woman very much until the couple announced their marriage. That's when the little girl started to act out and told the girlfriend she hated her.

The couple was stunned. They tried desperately to find out what caused such a dramatic change. When they finally got the little girl to open up about her feelings, she confessed that she was terrified of having a wicked stepmother like Cinderella had.

Not even people who were stepchildren themselves are prepared for the stepparent role. Just ask Laura Petherbridge, author, speaker, and founder of The Smart Stepmom ministry.[2] She thought she would have special insights into being a stepmother because she grew up as a stepchild. But any confidence she had quickly faded after a few months of being a stepmom. And now she has a ministry for women like her.

No matter who we are, no matter how wise we think we are, every stepparent needs help!

It seems like stepparents can't win, no matter what. If you're likeable, then loyalty to the biological parent is an issue. If your ways are different than expected—and they always are—then tradition is an issue. ("That's not the way *we* do things!") And if you're not perfect—and you definitely aren't—then all your flaws are scrutinized.

So don't worry if you feel like everything you do is wrong. Depending on what day it is and which family member you ask, you probably *don't* do anything right!

I get it. Being a stepparent is tough. There's no getting around it, but it's a little easier if you realize that stepparenting is a different kind of parenting.

There Is No "Stepparent's Day"

Okay, so there *is* an official Stepfamily Day on the calendar—along with Donut Day and Pancake Day—but I challenge you to find someone who celebrates it.

More than likely, you won't get a homemade card or a sentimental rose of recognition on a Sunday morning for being a stepparent. But that's not because you don't deserve it. We stepparents know that we've put in the work!

Still, we're only human, so it's easy to resent the lack of recognition and appreciation. After so many occasions of feeling like a failure, it's tempting to lash out, get even, or just give up, whether mentally or physically.

But I want to encourage you. Even though stepparenting is often a (very) difficult job with (very) little credit, you get the honor of planting seeds of love in the lives of the children you care for. And that's immensely important!

I hope you can allow yourself to see the value in the long-term investment. It's okay not to get credit. Jesus said that when you give, "do not let your left hand know what your right hand is doing, so that your giving may be in secret" (Matthew 6:3-4). In other words, give without expecting anything in return.

But that doesn't mean you won't ever be rewarded. Maybe no one else will notice, but God sees all—and He's in the blessing business! Immediately after Jesus told His followers to give in secret, He went on to add that "your Father who sees in secret will reward you" (Matthew 6:4).

I know it's hard to internalize those words on days when everyone in your family seems to be at each other's throats. It might not seem like anything good can come from your blended family when there's an awkward silent treatment waiting for you almost every night at the dinner table.

But every good thing you do in the name of Christ is making an impression on your stepchildren. They probably don't realize it in the moment, but in the long run, your care for them can pay off in ways you can't see and sometimes in ways you can't imagine.

Instead of measuring your success as a stepparent by how pleased your stepchildren appear, measure your success by seeking to honor God as best you can. God's love never wavers. You never have to worry what sort of mood He's in or if He plays favorites.

So keep fighting the good fight. Don't grow weary in doing good. And one day, you, too, will hear the phrase we all long to hear: "Well done, good and faithful servant" (Matthew 25:23).

It's Complicated

As I've said already, stepparenting is a different kind of parenting. The complicating factors of trauma and grief in most blended families are far beyond mere circumstances—they are troubles of the heart.

The more you know about the typical struggles of blended families, the more you can help your family members (and yourself) pinpoint the hurts and find healing.

I approached this chapter on stepparenting in a few different ways.

I want to help you grow in empathy for your stepfamily members. I want to help you walk in their shoes—to empathize with their pain and to better understand their fears.

More than anything, your stepchildren need your understanding. Especially if they are younger, they barely even understand themselves. They need you to help guide them through their confusing fears and emotions.

Too often we expect children to just float along on the waves of life. We don't anticipate their emotional reactions or illogical reasoning. Why is that? They are human, aren't they? They are immature, aren't they? Some kids still believe in Santa Claus, yet we expect them to intuitively understand that life is hard sometimes for no apparent reason. We expect them to conclude that life would be better if we all just got along.

Ain't gonna happen. Kids are kids. If they could take care of themselves, they wouldn't need parents. We have to help them process the times in their life when their world seems upside down.

In order to do that, parents have to feel what those kids feel and see life from their perspective. Then we need to help them make a broader, more long-term assessment of the situation.

That can't happen in a single, state-of-the-family-style talk. It takes weeks and months and sometimes years of listening, talking, asking questions, and even making decisions that the kids won't like because it's what's best for the family.

I want to help you recognize the troublesome areas of your life so that you can work *through* some of them and work *around* others. Living in a blended family can sometimes feel like walking through a field of land mines. Wouldn't it be nice if the soldiers had a map that shows where all the bombs are located? The map couldn't guarantee that no bombs would ever go off, but it would sure help!

And if a bomb did go off, at least the soldiers would have known it was a possibility and were prepared to assess the damage. It's much harder to come up with solutions if you can't even identify the problem.

I hope to help you understand that you're not alone in your struggles. Blended families have troubles—deep, heart-wrenching troubles. And at times it can feel hopeless, like you will never again experience happiness. But I'm here to tell you that others have gone through similar situations and come out on the other side. That assurance alone might give you the strength and courage you need to keep going. I know it helped me.

When I hear about the blessings that resulted from stepparents who persevered, it gives me hope that things aren't always as dark as they seem.

Know Your Stepchild

There are already countless books on parenting in general, so I won't address most of the more basic parenting strategies. But there is one particular strategy that biological parents seem to know instinctively, yet it is also one that many stepparents seem to miss. That strategy deals with *knowing* each of the children in your family.

If you have biological kids of your own, you know that each child is unique and views the world through different lenses. Those lenses depend on personality, disposition, and past experiences. Biological parents naturally see those personality differences taking shape day by day as their children grow and mature. Consciously and subconsciously, biological parents notice the ever-shifting changes in their children's personalities and characteristics.

The same influences of personality, disposition, and past experiences also affect your stepchildren. But stepparents don't have personal experience regarding how their stepkids have changed and grown. We have to acquire that knowledge through spending time with them.

It might sound counterintuitive, but it's important for stepparents to be friends with their stepchildren *first* before trying to behave like a "real" parent.

Stepchildren will often pull away from a stepparent who tries too soon to act like their parent. But they typically won't pull away from an adult who is simply trying to be their friend. Almost everyone—even children and teenagers—likes a person who is willing to listen to their stories.

For once, this is not as hard as it sounds. Study each child. Recognize the differences in their personalities. Get to know their likes and dislikes—favorite colors, movies, and styles. Learn what kinds of foods they like and don't like.

That way, when they are with you in the car or at the dinner table, you don't have to know exactly what to say. All you have to do is ask questions. Ask, then listen. Listen for the names of their friends (this tells you whom they trust). Listen for the names of teachers and coaches and pastors (this tells you whom they admire and look up to).

Most important, listen for emotional cues. This is crucial because recognizing emotional cues is like finding a trail of breadcrumbs to the child's heart. Kids will often drop hints to see if you really care, if you're really invested in their words. And you, in turn, can show that you care by asking related follow-up questions.

An emotional cue can often sound benign. Your stepchild might mention not feeling like doing a certain activity. He might talk about quitting a favorite sport, activity, or hobby; she might remark about how she hasn't been sleeping well. But if you're paying attention, these are all clues that point to an emotional root cause.

These sorts of clues call for the "three whys." This is a communication technique that helps a person get to the emotional reason behind certain attitudes or actions. It's not enough to ask, "Why do you want to quit baseball?" A child will often give a vague excuse, such as "I don't know. I just don't like it anymore."

You might follow up with, "I thought you loved baseball. Why don't you like it anymore?" To which he may answer, "I don't know." That's when you need to continue the conversation: "You must have a reason. Is there something going on at practice?"

"Well, I feel different from my friends."

"What makes you different from your friends?"

"Well, my mom isn't there at the games anymore. Everyone else's mother is there, and it makes me miss my mom."

And now you better understand what the child is going through.

Sometimes the child can't quite articulate the feeling, so the empathetic stepparent might need to offer suggestions that will help the child sort through the issue. This will likely require some trial and error, and it might sound something like "Do you feel different because your mom isn't there to watch your games anymore?"

This kind of emotional detective work gets easier as the stepparent gets to know the child and becomes a trusted friend.

Children will likely go through many different physical and emotional phases during your time as a blended family. Some will be specific to your stepfamily situation, while others are the result of the normal maturing process.

The level of friendship you're able to establish in the early years of your stepfamily will help define the relationship you'll have with those stepchildren for the rest of your life.

Stepchild by Default

Imagine having a jar full of pond water. Let's say that it's been sitting on the shelf for a while, so everything inside has settled. The dirt is on the bottom, the water is reasonably clear, and the microbes and maybe a couple of tadpoles are floating easily and carefree.

Now imagine picking up that jar and shaking it. What happens? Everything mixes together. The water is murky and unclear. The tadpoles and microbes are spinning around with no control over where they are going.

It's basically a mess, and even after you put the jar back on the shelf, it takes a while for everything to settle down again.

That's how children feel coming into a blended family. One moment everything was settled and reasonably familiar; the next moment their whole world is all mixed up.

What's more, they had little to no choice in any of it. They didn't get to vote on who Mom or Dad fell in love with. They didn't have various options of where to live or which other children would now be living with them.

The parents got to choose their new spouse, but the children didn't get to choose their new parent. While you were dating and preparing to patch two families together, your kids were largely clueless. They didn't know what blended-family life would be like.

The first couple of weeks might be okay or might be incredibly awkward as everyone tries to adjust. But then reality sets in and the kids start to panic. *Will it always be this way? Will anyone listen to me? Will it ever go back to the way it was before?*

Not all personalities get along. Not all new ways of life

are welcomed. And kids soon start to wonder if anyone cares what they think. They might have expressed their opinions when you were dating, but you chose this person as your spouse (and their stepparent) anyway. They probably feel like their concerns don't matter.

Yet if you're like many single parents, your children were the most important factor in your decision-making process. But do they know that? Have you ever told them? If not, it's important to sit down with your kids and share why you thought this person would work out best for the whole family, not just yourself. Kids need to know that they weren't merely an afterthought.

Even if the children aren't happy with the way their life is right now, they will still be comforted to know that you carefully considered their wellbeing. And that alone can make a positive difference in the home.

The Element of Grief

While we adults view remarriage with a renewed sense of hope and happiness, children often see it as the end of hope and happiness.

This is especially true for children of divorce. Many children of divorce quietly (or not so quietly) hope that their parents will get back together. Even if one of the spouses was abusive, children have a God-given love for their biological parents that rarely disappears completely.

Children often pray that God will heal their "bad" parent and make their mom and dad fall in love again. Children might even blame God as being uncaring or purposely cruel for not working fast enough to prevent the other parent from remarrying.

When a divorced parent remarries, the children must accept that the hope they had for their parents to reunite is gone. It's just one more loss that the children must endure.

In the case of a deceased parent, the children don't have the same hope that the parents will reunite, but they might hope that the surviving parent loved his or her spouse so much that a new marriage is out of the question.

Deep down they know that their parent might be lonely, yet it's still comforting to children to see evidence of some unending loyalty. Even when parents are blessed to have kids who are initially happy about the match, problems *always* appear out of nowhere like a wet fish to the face.

Robert and Rhonda are a typical couple who experienced this kind of surprise attack. They had known each other for years as family friends. In fact, Robert and his wife and Rhonda and her husband, along with all their kids, would often go skiing together.

Then, tragically, Robert's wife and Rhonda's husband both died of unrelated illnesses within eighteen months of each other.

At first things were a bit awkward between them, but they eventually started wondering why they shouldn't get married. They knew each other so well, after all, and their children seemed to support the idea.

Robert and Rhonda did lots of preparation work. They

talked to the kids, had family meetings, took classes, read information on blended families, and even took their families to a counselor for grief therapy.

By the time of their wedding day, everyone was excited and happy.

Then, like an atomic bomb, the fairy tale exploded. Because they were strong Christians, Robert and Rhonda were able to keep their marriage together, and they are certainly glad they did. But it was rough going for a while. You can read about their story in Robert's book, *When the Bottom Drops Out.*[3]

What was the cause of so much trouble? Robert's youngest son was thirteen when they married, and, without realizing it, Robert was treating his son preferentially over his wife. Robert fell victim to what I call "guilt parenting" (which I discuss in another chapter)—he was parenting out of the fear that the remarriage would have a negative impact on his son.

Demonstrating a preference for (or spoiling) one's biological children in order to "make up" for a remarriage is a common mistake in blended families. But giving in to kids' demands is not the right way to bring about healing.

The best way to handle the emotions associated with remarriage is to keep engaging with the children. Keep telling them how you had their best interests in mind from the beginning. Listen to their complaints but don't be taken hostage by their demands. And if your former spouse is deceased, assure the kids how much you loved their biological parent.

There is no easy way to assuage your children's feelings of

loss. The journey to genuine healing is one that takes a lot of time and communication.

Words They Don't Mean

Emotions cause kids—just like adults—to say things they don't mean. The book *With Those Who Grieve* is a compilation of interviews with people of all ages who have experienced devastating grief. One of those stories involves a young boy named Danny who told his best friend, Christopher, that he had cancer and was eventually going to die.

Christopher screamed "I hate you!" and ran home. But the dying boy had compassion and knew his friend was just sad, so Danny followed Christopher to his home.

This is Christopher's story in his own words:

I was on my bed crying, and the door opened. It was Danny and his mom. I yelled, "Get out, get out!"

Danny just stood there. "I hate you," I yelled at him. I hurt inside now when I think I yelled that. Danny didn't leave my room. He looked at his mom and I guess she just knew we had to be alone.

I kept yelling, "I hate you, I hate you, I hate you for dying." All Danny said was, "I know." And he picked up my baseball mitt, and came over by my bed. We were just quiet for a while. "I don't want to die," Danny said, "Honest." I felt crummy. Finally I said, "I don't hate you."

Danny said, "I know. Sometimes life just hurts."[4]

Isn't that the truth? Sometimes life just hurts and we don't know what to do. Kids do and say all sorts of things to make the emotional pain stop—they try to hurt themselves, threaten to run away, or numb the pain with addictive substances.

While we need to take their emotional state very seriously, it's also vital that we don't hold grudges or internalize those hurtful words. It's enough to know that sometimes life just hurts.

What's in a Name?

Like it or not, we put a lot of value on names. The grandma-naming frenzy, for example, shows how obsessed we are with naming. I'm hearing all these crazy grandma names like FiFi and Foxy and Tootsie—apparently because Grandma and its common derivatives sound too old.

I'm sorry, ladies, but you aren't going to change your age by changing your name!

Yet the value of a name makes sense when you think about it. Names indicate something. A last name declares what family you belong to, and a first name gives you a distinction, setting you apart from siblings. Finally, a title like Mom or Dad defines your role.

But when a stepparent comes onto the scene, no one's sure exactly what to call him or her.

Some successful stepfamilies have insisted that all their kids—both biological and step—refer to their married parents as Mom and Dad. This means that the kids potentially have two sets of people with those same titles. I think that works for some kids. Like mine, for example. Since they were just five and three when Robbie and I got married, I reminded them to call Robbie "Daddy" or "Dad" right away. They still call him that.

But my stepson Seth was already fourteen by the time we joined families. Instead of insisting that he call me "Mom," I asked him what he preferred to call me. He said he would rather call me by my first name. And I was fine with that. I'm not his mother, after all, and he was old enough to know and understand that.

If Seth had wanted to call me "Mom," I would have been thrilled, but I didn't want to compel him to call me something that wasn't in his heart. Why create yet another issue when there are already so many others to deal with?

I think William Shakespeare had it right: "A rose by any other name would smell as sweet."[5]

I've also heard about stepchildren who created special names for their stepparents. I also think that's great. It's a wonderful way for kids to bond with their new family member.

Whether it's your own name, a derivative of Mom or Dad, or even something that starts out as snarky but turns out cute, I think using the name that your stepchildren choose for you will give you more of a sense of belonging than anything you force them to call you.

Adoption

Last names are a different story. I already mentioned that a person's last name is a form of belonging. It says, *This is the tribe I belong to.* But what if a child's last name isn't the same as the mother or father he or she lives with? This is another way that stepchildren can feel like outsiders.

When Robbie and I married, my children were the only two Beasleys in a house of McDonalds. At least the children of divorced parents who live with their mother can usually still go to their father's house, where they share the same last name as the rest of the family. Yet the leader of my kids' Beasley tribe was gone. To which tribe did they belong?

It also bothered me that I had a different last name than my kids, especially since they no longer had a parent who shared their name. At one point, I could see the disappointment on my son's face when he started school with all its paperwork and roll calls. He realized, perhaps for the first time, that he was a Beasley, and I was a McDonald.

"You have a different last name than us?" he said.

After a couple years of marriage, Robbie and I decided we needed to pursue adoption so Benjamin and Katherine could be McDonalds just like the rest of the family.

At the same time, I didn't want to cut them off from David. He was such a good man that he deserved to have children who would carry on his name. So we decided to keep Beasley as an additional middle name.

Robbie and I spoke with his two boys about the adoption.

We wanted to get their thoughts and to talk to them about the ramifications of that decision. Adoption meant that Benjamin and Katherine would be treated like their blood brother and sister, including in matters of inheritance.

When we asked Seth, who was in high school at the time, he said, "It's fine with me. They already feel like my siblings anyway." I was so thankful for his gracious and loving attitude toward my children.

We also talked to David's family and told them our reasoning and our plan to keep Beasley in the kids' names. We made it clear that the Beasley family would forever be in our hearts and lives. They were thankful that the kids retained their family name, and they supported us throughout the adoption.

The adoption was a fairly easy decision for us. Between the death of their father and their young ages, adoption didn't change much at all in terms of our everyday lives. But if you are contemplating the adoption process, there are several factors you should consider:

The ages of the children matter. My kids were so young that I knew they would grow up feeling like Robbie was their daddy. It made sense for them to be adopted.

Seth, however, was fourteen when we got married and sixteen when Robbie adopted my kids. He would never think of me as his mother, so it didn't make sense.

The feelings of the kids should be considered. Talk to them about it. Do they like the idea?

Help them think through any issues they might have

overlooked. Is adoption a big deal to them? Is it a big deal to you? On a scale of one to ten, how would they rate the idea? What is the general feel of the conversation?

Consider what an adoption would mean in the long run, legally. For my children, it didn't change much. But for Robbie's kids, it meant sharing their inheritance with two additional siblings.

Might this cause problems in the future with your family? Will you need a will or a trust to help settle any disputes?

You might also need the agreement of the child's biological parent and/or family members. In our state, a biological parent has to sign a document giving up parental rights. Since in our case the biological parent was deceased, the paternal grandparent needed to sign over parental rights.

If my mother-in-law Joy hadn't loved Robbie so much, she never would have done it. In cases where the biological parent and/or grandparents aren't cooperative or friendly, this might be very difficult. So check the laws in your state concerning parental rights before initiating the process.

Adoption typically means that the name of the biological father or mother will no longer appear on the birth certificate. This was a hard decision for me. I didn't like the idea of erasing David's name from my children's birth certificates. He wanted more than anything to be a father, and now I was removing his name from the legal documents.

I even looked into the possibility of putting both names—Robbie and David—on the certificates, or at least having an asterisk with a note or something. But that wasn't an option with the government offices.

I asked myself what advice David would have given me. I knew almost immediately—David would have wanted them to be adopted. Yes, he wanted to be a father, but he also wanted his kids to have another father if he died prematurely.

The decision to adopt should never be taken lightly. In the end, *you* must decide what's best for your family. Pray and ask God to give you direction so that you can make the best decision with confidence.

The Importance of Respect

Another common problem in stepparenting is the issue of respect. When a child grows up with a parent, the expectation of respect is established from the beginning. Most humans have an innate understanding that our parents are authority figures and we are subject to their discipline.

But blended families don't come with a certificate granting that same understanding. Respect and authority aren't recognized automatically. Yes, you are an adult, and many children feel somewhat obligated to respect adults. But some kids—particularly teens and preteens—will rebel at the idea of having someone who's "not my parent" telling them what to do.

Many stepparents make things worse by either trying to assume the full role of a parent or going too far the other way and having virtually no relationship at all with their stepchildren. But there is a healthier place between those two extremes.

Just because you aren't a child's biological parent doesn't mean that you don't deserve respect and even love. Don't force that love, of course, but try to grow into it just like you would with any new relationship.

Think of yourself as a teacher or mentor. And in that role, you can certainly be a godly influence in your stepchildren's lives. As Titus 2:7-8 says, "Show yourself in all respects to be a model of good works, and in your teaching show integrity, dignity, and sound speech that cannot be condemned, so that an opponent may be put to shame, having nothing evil to say about us."

Your stepchildren aren't required to feel close to you, but they *do* need to respect your position, just as they would respect a teacher, mentor, or the parent of a friend.

I've heard stepchildren say that their stepparent doesn't deserve respect because he or she hasn't "earned" it. While there is a type of respect that's earned, such as admiration or reverence, there is another type of respect that comes with a person's position, such as police officer, school principal, or judge. The spouse of a parent is also a position—one that comes with its own measure of respect. Even if a child doesn't particularly like a stepparent, the child should honor that position simply out of respect for the biological parent.

There is also an expected level of respect for stepparents simply because they are fellow human beings. As a person made in God's image, you deserve common courtesy and consideration from your stepchildren. They don't have to love you—or even like you personally—but it's not too much to ask that they treat you just as well (or better) as they would treat a stranger on the elevator.

The biological parent should talk to his or her children about this issue as early as possible. But even if you've been married for a while and you've never had that talk with your biological kids, it's not too late.

This isn't simply a matter of discipline. It's about setting appropriate boundaries and levels of authority. It's about establishing how children are expected to treat the adults in their home. And you can't really expect kids to do something that's never been explained or clarified.

The Job of Discipline

Blended-family experts generally agree that discipline should primarily come from the biological parent. This was an area where I definitely made mistakes. When I married Robbie, I knew that my kids were undisciplined and in need of a masculine presence. And I made it clear that I wanted him to get my kids in line.

He did all right—but at great expense to his relationship with them.

My kids quickly became scared and confused. They barely knew who this man was, and suddenly he had authority over their lives. No other man had had that kind of authority. Why him?

Robbie would give an instruction, and my kids would ask "Why?" The more they asked, the more Robbie felt disrespected, and the cycle continued. By the time I resumed my role as my kids' primary disciplinarian, the damage was already done. Before my kids could ever form a healthy bond with Robbie, he had already scared the daylights out of them.

It took a long time for my kids to get over it. A couple of years passed before Katherine would even give Robbie a hug. She was much too scared. And to this day, Benjamin still slinks away when he detects a hint of frustration in Robbie's voice.

For the sake of your children, the biological parent should establish the expectations of authority. Tell your kids what words and actions are and are not respectful. Explain who has the final say when instructions are conflicting. Give them a specific explanation of how the rules in your family will work.

And when punishments are doled out, let them come from the biological parent. Even when biological parents are "mean," their kids still know that they are loved. But a stepparent has to gain their trust. So let the biological parent be the bad guy.

No Perfect Answers

These are only a few of the stepparenting lessons I've picked up along the way. That said, there is no perfect answer for every situation. The best thing you can do, no matter what

PARENTING
AND GUILT

WHAT HAVE I DONE TO MY CHILDREN?

I can't remember when I first asked myself that question, but it haunts me to this day. I see the mistakes I made. I see the pain my children suffered along the way, and I still wonder how things might have been different if David hadn't died.

The nagging fear of my kids being traumatized first appeared the moment I heard David was dead. Within moments, all the articles and statistics I'd read about the influence of father figures flooded my mind.

My questions were overwhelming: *Who will teach Benjamin to be a man? Where will Katherine get her example of a godly husband? Will they truly know how much their father loved them?*

From that point on, every mistake I made and every emotional explosion that poured out of me provided yet another opportunity for me to feel guilty about my parenting skills (or lack thereof). And there were plenty of opportunities.

I think about all the times I sat motionless for who knows how long, lost in my thoughts. The depth of the sadness I experienced made a grieving parent like me forget the world outside. And that outside world included my kids.

I don't mean that grieving parents forget they *have* kids. But grief has a way of making a person go inward. It's like being hypnotized. I'll never forget the time I snapped out of a thought trance to see my eighteen-month-old daughter climbing the shelves in the fridge to get her own snack and one for her brother.

Poor Katherine was just tired of saying, "Mom, Mom, Mom," without a response while I was zoned out in my grief. I hadn't intentionally ignored her, but I doubt she could recognize that. Did she know if I cared whether she was hungry or not?

Those were the kind of thoughts that haunted me. Time after time, the inner voices of guilt condemned me.

If I was a better parent, my children wouldn't be so frustrated all the time. They were never this way before David's death.

These school grades are pretty bad. If their dad was still alive, this wouldn't happen.

Our life is so chaotic now. I never was good at details. That was David's job. I'm such a failure.

That's what it's like when guilt is running the show. I call it guilt-driven parenting.

Doing It Alone

Robbie always said being a single dad was easier than being a single mom. His theory is that most people assume the dad has a harder time caring for kids, cooking, and doing housework. As a result, dads get a lot more help (and grace).

Single moms, however, get no slack. We're expected to do it all and do it flawlessly.

All moms (single or not) face peer pressure to be the best mother in the world. There's an unspoken standard that we should be germ-free, party-planning, game-playing, cookie-baking Betty Crockers, who are as pretty as we are nice. (Just like Betty Crocker is a fictional character, so is the idea of this perfect mother.)

That's an impossible standard for any mother, but for a single mom it's just ridiculous. It's like expecting a one-legged pack mule to carry you up Mount Everest. Single moms just don't have the resources or the time!

People have different expectations for single moms versus single dads, but the reality is the same for both—you can't do it all by yourself. You were never *meant* to do it all by yourself. Parenting was designed to be a two-person job.

Yet single parents have no choice but to fill all the roles at home—both mother and father. Both disciplinarian and comforter. Strong enough to provide safety and soft enough to express sympathy. Single parents are stuck in a situation where failure is bound to happen.

Then there's the emotional roller coaster.

Emotions can make a person go haywire. We turn into ticking time bombs. The slightest irritation can make a hurting person blow up. There will be yelling, blaming, and sobbing.

And when we blow up, we know we were probably somewhat right *and* somewhat wrong. But we don't know how to explain that to our children, especially younger kids. ("I'm sorry for some things, but not for others.") That's a hard concept for kids—and many parents—to sort out.

There are days when grief, anxiety, sorrow, and frustration feel overwhelming to a parent, and there is nothing the poor kids can do about it! You'll often find these emotional victims staring into space, overcome by tears for seemingly no reason.

When the mind and the soul are suffering, the body is too. Grief suppresses the immune system to the point that everything hurts. Muscles are tight and sore from tension and stress. Sleep is erratic. Viruses and headaches are more common.

The hurting person craves rest, both mentally and physically. We tell ourselves, *Leave the dishes, forget the clothes, warm up some nuggets—I'm exhausted!*

But even when grieving parents feel depleted, we still love our children and want the best for them. That's when single parents get stuck in two ruts: doing what's easy and making kids happy.

Establishing Bad Patterns

An emotionally stable adult knows that "make your children happy" is a terrible parenting goal. First of all, most kids will never reach a state of constant contentment. They always want *more*.

They have little understanding of the value of money, time, or sacrifice. They are just kids, after all, so they haven't learned these concepts yet. That's why kids have parents.

Single parents experience life in survival mode. We (often wrongly) give in to the wishes of our kids for many of the reasons I mentioned earlier: exhaustion, wanting a moment of peace, or guilt. Then we justify it by telling ourselves, *It's only this once,* or *Maybe this will make up for yelling earlier.*

What we don't realize, however, is that we're establishing patterns in our children's lives. Studies show that if you do an action every day for two weeks in a row, it becomes a habit. Well, kids pick up on those habits too. They especially pick up on habits that get them what they want!

As a single father, Robbie could see that his attitude and behavior was affecting his teenage son, but he didn't know how to fix it. So he did what many single fathers do—he gave Seth plenty of money and tried to give him most everything he wanted.

That was all Robbie knew to do. It seemed to make Seth happy, and it made Robbie feel like a good father to make Seth happy.

Another tradition that Robbie started was a daily after-school trip to the drive-thru to get dinner. Seth expected that tradition to continue with our blended family, but I didn't feel the same way. Not only did I think the meals were unhealthy, I was also concerned about the cost. (By the time I bought something for all three kids after every school day, it came out to several hundred dollars a month!)

It wasn't Seth's fault that his dad created this expectation, and to cut it off suddenly and permanently seemed like the quickest path to becoming the wicked stepmother. So I let it go on for a year.

By the time the next school year began, I'd decided that a full meal was too much. After all, Seth got his drive-thru dinner around three thirty, and the rest of us sat down together for a family meal at five o'clock. Unsurprisingly, most nights Seth opted not to join us because he wasn't hungry.

So that next school year, I agreed to buy the kids just a snack. That tradition continued for another year or so until Seth started driving himself to and from school.

The choice to continue the after-school tradition required a monetary compromise for me, but it was a small price to pay to help Seth have a smoother transition into our blended family. I wanted him to feel seen and important. I couldn't accommodate everything he wanted—nor should I have—but this was a relatively minor thing that was certainly doable. So I did it.

During my time as a guilt-ridden single mom, my kids were too young to care about money. But they did care about television and food choices. I sometimes made myself feel better by letting my preschool-age son make choices for the three of us.

Want hot dogs for dinner for the tenth day in a row? *Okay with me if it brings some peace.* Want to watch the same preschool program over and over, all day every day? *Looks like a good show to me.*

Guess what the kids expected to do when Robbie and I got married?

Robbie and I had created expectations and patterns in our children. He taught Seth, and I taught Benjamin, that the household revolved around their desires.

This is just one example of the consequences of guilt-driven parenting. Children of single parents end up learning bad habits and patterns in lots of other ways.

Many times, kids brought up in single-parent homes don't get the discipline they need. Single parents are tired, confused, and often outnumbered. By evening, after working all day, most of them don't have much fight left. So they give in to the kids' wishes and swear it's "only this one time."

In turn, children of single parents often take on adult roles. They might become their parent's confidant or emotional support. And that's not good because children don't have the wisdom or the maturity to help their parents. They weren't meant to take on the burdens of adult life. The pressure of these expectations can make them feel emotionally overwhelmed and insecure.

Children of single parents often learn to take care of themselves. That's not all bad—kids certainly need to learn life skills—but becoming independent too soon may give them a false sense of confidence that leads to risky behaviors.

Of course, when single parents are in survival mode, we excuse the bad habits we've encouraged in our kids. We tell ourselves, *It won't always be this way.* Perhaps we fantasize about the day when we'll be married again in a happy blended family—a family where everyone loves and enjoys each other. We imagine laughter ringing in our ears and sparkles in everyone's eyes.

But fantasy and reality are different worlds.

Along Comes Stepfamily

When a blended family comes together, all those shortcuts we took as single parents suddenly come back to bite us. The joy we anticipated about the prospect of a two-parent home quickly fades, replaced by the sounds of unhappy children.

A big reason why many single parents get remarried is to help fill the gaps created by the missing parent. So, when kids are disappointed and unhappy, the guilt reappears and begins to choke out all the good intentions and unrealistic expectations you had during the engagement period.

That's when guilt becomes less of an annoyance and more like a cancer—eating the family alive. And that's when parents start pondering all the past situations when we *should have* done things differently.

I remember how guilty I felt when Robbie and Benjamin weren't getting along. All the *should haves* flooded my mind. I *should have* let Robbie spend more time with my kids, getting to know them, and vice versa. I *should have* waited longer to get married. Maybe I *should have* married someone else.

Robbie, meanwhile, empathized with his confused teenage son. Seth lost his regular Saturday golf games. He lost the freedom to eat fast food every day. He sometimes felt punished, picked on, and overlooked.

Robbie had another struggle with guilt that he wasn't expecting. He felt bad for spending too much time with my kids. My children were so much younger than his, and they longed to make their new daddy laugh, so they climbed on his back and soaked up his attention.

Robbie's biological children were older and more independent, so he didn't get to spend as much time with them or as often. This caused a loyalty crisis in Robbie's heart. He didn't want his own kids to think he loved them less than mine.

All these issues eat away at a parent's emotions. It's torturous to enter a situation that you think will make everyone happy—especially after experiencing so much sorrow—and find out that it only made things worse!

All those questions, all those what-ifs, ultimately lead to feelings of regrets. And for many of us, regrets are hard to ignore and even harder to resist.

I appreciate what authors William and Patricia Coleman say about regrets:

> Regrets are hard to argue with. Who can find a time when we were perfect? We could have done more. We could have done better. We could have given it one more try. Regrets are like stars. There will always be plenty to count. When someone dies, there is always more we could have said; there are more times when we could have been there; there is more time we could have devoted to prayer; there are more hours we could have spent by the bed. Any attempt to dissuade us of this would only fall on deaf ears. Regrets can be tossed away only by their owner.[1]

Because regrets always seem to win the argument, we parents start allowing them to steer our parenting decisions. In our attempts to make a situation better, we end up making some very common mistakes.

Making Excuses

Perhaps the most common mistake is excusing bad behavior in our children. There's a natural tendency in parents and grandparents to feel sorry for children who've lost a parent or gone through a difficult divorce, so we let them get away with some stuff. And it's not too long before some stuff becomes a lot of stuff.

I'm not sure why we make excuses for poor behavior. Maybe it's because we're like Adam, who blamed Eve for his own sin. If we can come up with something or someone else to blame, we don't have to be responsible for trying to change the behavior.

After all, if we acknowledge the behavior, then we have to do something about it. And that's hard. It often seems easier to simply live with the problems than try to fix them. But when we overlook the wrongs rather than address them, we're forcing others to live with the bad behavior too.

Yes, children *will* face difficulties resulting from their parents' grief or a remarriage. But they can also learn from those experiences. Even though the experiences may be bad, the outcomes can still be good.

But if we use grief as an excuse for poor behavior, our children can suffer even greater consequences as they grow. I knew this was a bad tendency, yet I *still* caught myself explaining, "Well, you see, Benjamin lost his father, so he . . ."

Kids pick up on those kinds of excuses and use them against parents. That doesn't mean they are necessarily bad kids—just human. Children naturally manipulate the feelings of parents and other authority figures to get what they want—just like most of us have done.

If you find yourself making the excuse that your children endured a traumatic event, then your children will likely use that same excuse against you and other adults, such as teachers. And they won't learn to live a disciplined life.

The Blame Game

Another habit of guilt-driven parenting is the tendency to blame problems on the stepparent. If life before the blended family formed was relatively smooth sailing, then it stands to reason that the tough times that came after are the fault of your new spouse, right?

Wrong.

There are all kinds of issues contributing to problems in a blended family. We've already discussed many of them. Forming a stepfamily is a lot like one of those reality TV shows that puts a bunch of strangers on an island to see how well they can handle life together. There is always drama!

Sure, your new spouse has probably made some mistakes, but so has everyone else in the family. Your children certainly aren't blameless, and neither are you.

I once heard a very helpful strategy for remarried couples trying to work out their problems. It's a simple way to engage in conversation without blaming one another, and I'll share it with you: The couple sits on a couch, side by side, with a pillow in a chair across from them. The pillow represents the problem, and sitting on the couch together represents that the couple is on the same side, working together to accomplish a goal. Putting the pillow across from them is a visual reminder to focus on the *problem* instead of each other. Give it a try the next time you work through a family issue.

Keep in mind that a blended family is a broken family by

definition. And with brokenness comes problems. You need to expect friction, disagreements, hurt feelings, and grief. According to Ron Deal, it takes an average of five to seven years for your stepfamily to finally feel like a family.[2] That's also the typical point when many remarried couples give up. Five to seven years seems like a long time to live with frustration, but if you can learn to compromise and work together, life *does* get better.

You Live Your Life, I'll Live Mine

Guilt sometimes causes parents to put the needs of their biological children ahead of their new spouse. This is often done unintentionally, but the couple might end up deciding that living like two separate families under one roof is easier.

In this scenario, Mom takes care of her kids, and Dad takes care of his kids. She handles her finances, and he handles his. This arrangement might make things seem easier in the short term, but it only reinforces the idea that compromise and family bonding aren't possible. It creates an invisible barrier between the two groups and prevents new family relationships from forming.

It also creates competition and jealousy among stepsiblings. "Dad's kids get more money than we do!" "Why does Johnny get to play baseball and I don't?"

In addition to dividing the kids, this type of stepfamily also divides the couple. It hinders bonding in the marriage relationship, and without a strong marriage foundation, the blended family likely won't make it for the long haul.

The Marriage Comes First

A strong marriage, even a remarriage, between a man and a woman provides the best environment for kids to thrive. A healthy marriage is the best way to nurture all your children, helping them grow to be emotionally, spiritually, and physically strong.

In a study titled "Why Marriage Matters for Child Wellbeing," professor David C. Ribar concludes:

> [S]tudies of child wellbeing . . . typically find that direct positive associations remain between children's wellbeing and marriage, strongly suggesting that marriage is more than the sum of [its] particular parts. . . . The advantages of marriage for children's wellbeing are likely to be hard to replicate through policy interventions other than those that bolster marriage itself.[3]

Ribar's conclusions are consistent with biblical principles of child-rearing and family: Healthy marriages produce healthy children.

All children, even adult children, need to know their parents are okay. Until kids are convinced that a new spouse is here to stay, they feel responsible for their own parent's wellbeing. When they see unity forming between you, it gives them a sense of security knowing that Mom or Dad will be okay.

A strong remarriage relationship will also help prepare your children for their future marriage. Marriage doesn't come with an owner's manual. Most young people get their ideas about marriage based on what they saw in their home. Kids learn to be adults by watching adults—predominantly their parents. And when you have a good marriage, you are teaching your kids to have one too.

This is especially important for children of divorced parents. Your first marriage might have been rife with struggles and maybe even abuse. If your ex-spouse has remarried, your kids will also be watching the way that other marriage works.

I heard about a stepmom who had a hard time bonding with her stepchildren. No matter what she did, the kids didn't like her, especially the teenage daughter. Years later, when the stepdaughter was grown and married, she sent a letter to her stepmother, thanking her for being an example of a godly wife.

The stepdaughter, now a wife herself, realized that what she saw modeled through her father and stepmother's marriage was a far better way of life than what she learned from her biological mother and stepfather.

Finally, a strong marriage is vital because you are modeling the gospel through your roles as husband and wife. In Ephesians 5:22-33, the apostle Paul explains how marriage is a living example of Christ's relationship with the church. Husbands should love wives with the kind of sacrificial love that Jesus demonstrated, and wives are to emulate how the church honors Christ and follows His leading.

Even a remarriage can show kids how to have healthy communication, forgiveness toward one another, commonalities, friendship, and mutual trust. They may not realize it now, but one day your children will likely have families of their own, and you will see the seeds you sowed produce fruit in their lives.

Remember, Kids Leave

Several chapters ago I recounted how my young son asked me if I loved Robbie more than him. "When you're all grown up and married someday," I told him, "Robbie will be here with me. And you will be on your own."

That was a moment of clarity for both my son and me.

Children are only with us for a brief time, and while we have a grand responsibility to raise them in God's ways, He didn't intend for them to stay with us forever. We are to train them to be strong, self-sufficient adults who love the Lord, and then send them off into the world like arrows. Psalm 127:4 says, "Like arrows in the hand of a warrior are the children of one's youth."

Some mothers devote all their time and affection to their kids, but eighteen years later those same moms are lost. They might even feel betrayed or try to cling to and control their adult children.

This same attitude shows up in blended families. Kids are (often unwitting) experts at manipulating our affections with accusations and predictions, and a parent's love tempts us to side with our children when there is family tension.

After all, we've known our children longer and gone through significant, life-altering times together.

But if you want a healthy, stable blended-family home, you must learn the value of supporting your spouse. That does not include, however, supporting an abusive person. I'm certainly not advocating that you sacrifice your children on the altar of your marriage. Even if your spouse isn't abusive, you might still have occasion to reprimand him or her for unhealthy displays of anger or frustration. (After all, none of us is perfect.)

Yet, in general, a united front is the best option in a healthy family situation. This exemplifies the spiritual importance of the marital relationship and God's hierarchy for families. Jesus said that a house divided against itself cannot stand (Mark 3:25). And even if you've been previously divorced, God still wants you to remain with your current spouse "till death do us part." Your children will move on someday, but if you drive a wedge between you and your spouse, your marriage will eventually fail.

The day I took a strong stand with my son was the day I drew a line in the sand. I essentially told Benjamin, "Robbie is my spouse, and you are not."

Ben is fifteen now, and he loves Robbie. He respects him; he's proud of him. But most important, he sees his mother and father as a united force.

After about five years of marriage, Ben stopped pushing me to choose between him and Robbie. He figured out that it was a losing battle.

That wasn't easy for me. I shed a lot of tears when Ben couldn't see how my loyalty to Robbie was actually good for him. But each tear watered seeds of stability in our lives, and we are now reaping the benefits.

Every time I hear "Watch, Dad!" or see Ben happy when he's pleased Robbie, I say a little prayer of thanksgiving.

Life Is Pain

There are several quotes about life in the movie *The Princess Bride*. One in particular, from the Dread Pirate Roberts/ Westley, is quite insightful for stepfamilies: "Life *is* pain, Highness. Anyone who says differently is selling something."[4] (Clearly the pirate life has similarities to blended-family life.)

But long before Westley professed his love to Buttercup, Jesus gave us a similar warning: "In the world you will have tribulation" (John 16:33). Your children will suffer tribulation in your stepfamily. They are already suffering from the loss of a previous family. But Jesus tells us that no one lives life without suffering. God has promised us, however, that through the suffering, He has overcome.

The apostle Paul told us to rejoice in our sufferings. He wrote, "We rejoice in our sufferings, knowing that suffering produces endurance, and endurance produces character, and character produces hope, and hope does not put us to shame, because God's love has been poured into our hearts through the Holy Spirit" (Romans 5:3-5).

We all want our children to display endurance, character, hope, and the evidence of God's love poured into their hearts through the Holy Spirit. We read about all the good things that suffering produces, yet we still try to insulate them from every minor twinge of pain.

Here's another reason to embrace suffering: James 1:2-4 tells us to "count it all joy, my brothers, when you meet trials of various kinds, for you know that the testing of your faith produces steadfastness. And let steadfastness have its full effect, that you may be perfect and complete, lacking in nothing."

While we certainly don't look forward to suffering, blended-family life is nonetheless an opportunity for our children to experience various trials. They will likely look at life and ask the hard questions, and it's only by asking those questions that they can discover life-changing answers.

That's why you shouldn't let guilt compel you to protect your children from every form of suffering. Sure, one of the jobs a parent has is to protect, yet I think that's where we get confused about letting children suffer. The suffering that Scripture is talking about here is not the kind that puts a child in danger. This kind of suffering is more like a struggle.

By allowing your children to struggle and face trials, you are helping them grow stronger under your loving supervision. Don't try to take away all their pain. Help them grow stronger through it.

God Has a Plan

No one loves your children more than God does. God gave your children to you. He knew that you would all be going through these circumstances together, and He has already planned how you're going to get through them.

Let's look at the story of Joseph, beginning in Genesis 37. Joseph was hated by his half brothers, who sold him into slavery. He ended up in Egypt where he was falsely accused of rape and landed in prison.

Joseph suffered a lot! But through God's sovereign plan, Joseph eventually became the second most powerful man in all Egypt. A terrible drought came, but because of Joseph's leadership, the people had stored up enough food to provide for the entire kingdom.

By this point, Joseph was a trusted and respected leader. People came to Egypt from many surrounding lands, all seeking relief from the drought. And wouldn't you know it, his half brothers also showed up in search of help.

They didn't realize at first that they were talking to Joseph, but he finally revealed himself. This was the brother they had sold into slavery! They were terrified! But do you know what Joseph said to them? "As for you, you meant evil against me, but God meant it for good" (Genesis 50:20).

Joseph followed God, and he could now see the plan God had laid out for his life. He didn't blame his brothers. He didn't take out his revenge. He embraced all he had gone through, knowing that God was using it for good.

This story reflects the principle found in Romans 8:28: "And we know that for those who love God all things work together for good, for those who are called according to his purpose."

The future is in God's hands. Trust Him with your children's futures. With your stepchildren's futures. Trust that God can use any trauma they experience for good in their lives. Besides, you can't make it all go away, so don't spend your days worrying about it.

When you feel like you are being controlled by emotions, either yours or your child's, seek the Lord in prayer and let the Scriptures be your guide. There is so much in the Bible about why we can and should trust God.

You are not in as much control as you think. Children aren't robots—they can't be programmed to produce the outcomes you want. They have a will, and they make decisions. As parents, we can do our best to follow Scripture and point our children to God, but our kids are ultimately responsible for their own lives. Guilt-driven parenting won't make family life any better, and in most cases, it will make it worse.

So stop worrying. Pray, do your best, and let God take care of the rest!

HELPING KIDS
PROCESS EMOTION

AUTHOR AND THEOLOGIAN James R. White wrote, "Everyone old enough to love is old enough to grieve."[1] Grief is a deep wound in a child's soul. Even when we parents do our best to keep wounds from occurring, we can't make the scars go away. And they will likely be there for the rest of our children's lives.

That sounds so tragic. Many of us know what it's like to live with scars. They remind us that life isn't perfect. They remind us of past pain. And sometimes they hurt for no reason at all, even long after they've healed.

But scars aren't all bad. Scars tell a story. They represent the things we've survived.

Aren't you grateful for the scars that Jesus bears? When Jesus came out of the grave, God could have made His scars disappear. But for the sake of those who needed proof of Christ's crucifixion and resurrection, God left them there. The disciple Thomas was one of those who wanted evidence. He said he wouldn't believe Jesus had risen until he could see Jesus' wounds for himself.

So the risen Jesus appeared to Thomas and said, "Put your finger here, and see my hands; and put out your hand, and place it in my side. Do not disbelieve, but believe" (John 20:27).

God didn't take away Jesus' scars, and He doesn't take away our scars for much the same reason. Scars tell the story of love, loss, and life renewed.

According to counseling professors Alicia Skinner Cook and Kevin Ann Oltjenbruns, "Grief is an individual's way of regaining balance and of restoring a sense of equilibrium in one's life."[2]

In other words, processing emotional wounds requires getting to the point where a stepchild can accept the losses caused by this new life and adjust. Stepchildren must learn how they fit into a blended family and accept the situation as one that includes many good things.

For Christians, processing emotional wounds also offers the opportunity to share burdens, love unconditionally, and strengthen godly character. This chapter will discuss how to help the hurting children in your family with compassion and grace.

Embracing the Memories

It's vital to be available when hurting children want to talk about their memories or their emotions. You don't have to force conversations or announce, "Now it's time to talk about your mother." Don't make it like some kind of formal counseling session. Just get them talking.

These conversations can take place in the car after school, out running errands, or while fixing a snack in the kitchen. Just bring up the subject from time to time. If they don't want to talk at the moment, that's okay. Even if they don't want to talk right away, you've still let them know that it's okay to bring it up. You're willing to have a conversation when they are ready.

Kids are sometimes reluctant to talk about their biological parent because they don't want to hurt feelings or make others feel uncomfortable. For kids whose parents are divorced, they may not want to say that they love their biological parent more. They might not want Mom or Dad to be upset by how much they think about the other parent. Maybe they believe that talking about the biological parent isn't welcome.

For children who've lost a parent to an accident or illness, they might feel self-conscious about admitting their sadness. Our society often treats death like a creepy subject that only morbid people want to discuss. Your kids need to know that it's completely natural and normal to talk about dear loved ones who have passed away.

Not many generations ago, we lived in a world where

death was a regular part of life. A large portion of the population raised animals and killed them with their own hands to provide food for their family. Nowadays, most of our food is processed for us, so we are shielded from this natural process.

The Disney television series *Liv and Maddie* included a scene that describes this perfectly. Teenage brothers Joey and Parker are having a discussion when Joey responds, "It's like believing that fried chicken comes from real chickens."[3] Of course, he was appalled when he found out that they actually do!

All of us, including Christians, have become accustomed to trying to make our current lives on earth longer and more comfortable. But life on this earth will never be our best life. On earth we live with death and pain. The Christian's best life is the one that comes after our days on earth are over.

Some people think children should be shielded from the topic of death, but if you don't talk to kids about what they've experienced, they'll have little choice but to make up their own explanations. This was emphasized by Elyse Fitzpatrick and Jessica Thompson in their book *Answering Your Kids' Toughest Questions*:

> We should not try to shield our children from knowing about it nor should we try to avoid talking about it. We really can't shelter our children from the knowledge of death, no matter how we might want to. All our children need do is walk outside and see a dead bug, watch a leaf fall from a tree,

or see a patch of dead grass to know that death is, in fact, the one constant in all of life.[4]

The Bible itself never shies away from addressing tough topics like death or divorce. Our faith helps us face the hard problems in life with real answers—the only answers that really work. Once again, Fitzpatrick and Thompson provide insightful thoughts:

> The Christian faith does not portray an unrealistic world where everything is perfect, nor does it avoid addressing the painful, hard-to-understand things of life. Christianity is for real people with real problems. Out of all the world's religions, ours is the only one that deals with death in a hope-giving yet realistic way.[5]

That doesn't mean children need to know the gruesome details of a parent's death or all the hardships of a previous difficult marriage. I told my children that David died of blunt force trauma as a result of a head-on collision. But I haven't told them specifics about the accident or shown them the pictures taken at the scene. I can always show them the images, if they are interested, when they are older.

Children just need to know that with Jesus we can always face the truth, even when it's hard. No matter what we've been through, He can help us overcome any adversity that comes our way.

Don't Take Their Grief Away

It's hard to see a child sad. No one enjoys the tears of a little one. We want to comfort them and say things like "There, there. Everything will be okay. Stop crying." We want to take away their sorrow and make them happy again.

But please don't try to quash or suppress your children's emotions. Remember the story of the mother who said, "Don't take my grief from me"? Children also need to have their sadness validated. Embrace their pain. You can assure them that everything will be okay someday, but don't make them feel bad about their tears.

Kids need to know it's okay to express their emotions. They need to feel sad and express that sadness. It's a form of honoring the person they have lost. Yet most of the messages they receive discourage those feelings.

The authors of *When Children Grieve* cite a study that determined "by the time a child is fifteen years old, he or she has already received more than twenty-three thousand reinforcements that indicate that it is not acceptable to show or communicate about sad feelings."[6]

Children need to feel permission to miss a parent, to dislike a family situation, or to express other grievances. Those feelings probably won't change the situation, but that's okay. Changing their circumstances is not the goal. It's the expression of their feelings and the validation of those feelings that really helps.

Once again, don't tell grieving children to just "move on."

Most of the time, people who say that are trying to be helpful. What they're trying to communicate is "It's not healthy to be depressed all the time. I want you to be happy again." They have good intentions, but their words have the opposite effect. Telling someone to "move on" sounds like you are telling them to forget the person they loved or to stop missing them.

When a parent or stepparent misunderstands grief and discourages it, children might resent being encouraged to leave their previous family situation behind. The new marriage might already seem to the child as an encouragement to forget.

But we don't move on from people we love; we simply learn *how* to miss them. As children continue to mature, the sadness of past memories will lessen while the happiness from those same memories grows. Kids should feel free to discuss feeling sad and the losses they've endured for as long as those feelings persist.

A Christian's role includes having compassion on those who are hurting, even when you might have played a part in their pain. As Paul said, "If one member suffers, all suffer together; if one member is honored, all rejoice together" (1 Corinthians 12:26).

The key is not to smooth over their grief but to acknowledge it. Galatians 6:2 tells us, "Bear one another's burdens, and so fulfill the law of Christ." Talk to your stepchildren about missing their parent. Laugh at their stories and cry with their tears.

Emotional pain also has the potential to bring children into a closer relationship with God. When His children are hurting, God is a healer and a comforter. Just like a spouse who remains by the bedside of a seriously ill husband or wife, God remains closer than ever. Even when children become angry at God, allow them to ask questions and direct their frustrations at the Lord. He will always offer comfort.

In his book *Don't Waste Your Sorrows*, author and pastor Paul Billheimer writes, "Until one is broken, he is full of himself, his plans, his ambitions, his value judgements. One is often so full of self that there is little room for more of God."[7]

In a world where many kids have learned to focus on self more than anything else, it's important to let God do His work in the broken hearts of children.

Signs of Grief

If you've experienced grief yourself, you probably don't need a list of the signs. You already understand many of the different ways that grief can show up.

But if you've not experienced a deep personal loss of your own, it helps to know that the emotions you observe in children aren't always what they seem. Often the fears, anger, and stress you see in your kids are fueled by feelings of unrest and loss stemming from the loss of a parent—as well as the changes brought on by the forming of a blended family.

One quick warning, however: Children can figure out how to use these feelings as a way to manipulate their parents. Author, widow, and college professor Judith Fabisch tells the story of an eleven-year-old boy who blamed his depressing day on missing his dad, who had died three years earlier. "An honest evaluation of the situation," Fabisch writes, "revealed that his play for sympathy revolved around the fact that he didn't want to clean his room."[8]

Dr. Kay Soder-Alderfer is a counselor, writer, and speaker who often focuses on issues of grief. In her book *With Those Who Grieve*, she offers this list of ways that grief can affect people physically, mentally, emotionally, socially, or spiritually:[9]

Physical
- loss of appetite
- weight gain or loss
- sleeping problems
- frequent headaches
- vision problems
- fatigue
- loss of balance
- addiction

Mental
- difficulty concentrating
- forgetfulness
- memory loss
- nightmares
- depression
- confusion

Emotional
- numbness
- anger
- loneliness
- emptiness
- abandonment
- guilt
- fear
- feeling overwhelmed
- stress

Social
- isolation
- avoiding places attached to memories
- only wanting to spend time in places with memories
- staying home when the family goes out
- making new friends and abandoning old ones
- refusing to make new friends or try new things
- workaholism
- clinging to familiar social patterns and customs

Spiritual
- thoughts of death
- questioning previously held beliefs
- finding new meaning in God
- feeling abandoned or punished by God
- turning away from God
- becoming more reflective on spiritual matters

- displaying anger at God
- questioning the meaning of life

You'll notice that many of the items on the list seem contradictory. That's because everyone grieves differently. Children often don't have the words to express their emotions, so those emotions come out in their actions. *I'm Grieving as Fast as I Can* author Linda Feinberg says, "Think about what it would be like if, instead of having the power of speech, you were forced to play a game of charades for everything you wanted to say."[10] Communication can feel like that for kids!

Look for differences or changes in a child's personality. Biological parents will usually have an advantage in noticing such changes, but what about stepparents? How can you notice atypical reactions or changes in personality if you didn't know the child before you became a blended family?

Get to know your stepchildren as much as they will let you.

Grieving the Parent They Live With

Children don't grieve only the parent who's no longer around. They also grieve the loss of the parent they live with. Wait, what? It's true. You might not be gone physically, but you're no longer the same person you were prior to your blended family. Your time, attention, and resources are now spread thinner with the addition of new family members.

The result is that your own kids now get less of you. They may also get less money or gifts on holidays and birthdays.

Your regular routines like bedtime or favorite pastimes might be altered or reduced. It's tough for kids to give up existing family habits, traditions, and expectations. They will grieve those losses.

The bond between single parents and their kids often grows deeper because they've been through a traumatic event together. Those difficult times can strengthen loyalties between family members. And in a single-parent home, kids typically have more input. Single parents usually give more attention to their children and even include them in family decisions, like what to have for dinner. They get to have an opinion about what to watch on TV or how to spend family time together.

It's not a great idea for single parents to create these kinds of expectations in their children. Kids should be treated like kids, not equals. But the truth is that single parents sometimes find it easier to just let someone else make decisions for a change.

That pattern usually comes back to bite Mom or Dad, though, especially in a blended family. That's because when a new family forms, parents put their children back into the category of being "just kids." Any special attention subsides, and while the adults might feel as though this is no big deal, the kids probably won't agree.

It's hard for children to understand why everything happens the way it does in a blended family. A child might wonder, *How could my father/mother do this to me? Doesn't he/she love me? Wasn't I enough?*

Just like adults, kids resent being "put in their place." This is especially true for older siblings who had previously adopted more of an adult role after a death or divorce.

Older children typically have more responsibility and become much closer to their biological parent during the single-parenting season. A daughter might feel a sense of pride that her father needs her now more than ever. A son might feel like the man of the house. But when that single parent remarries, many of those roles are taken over by the new spouse, resulting in possible jealousy and resentment among older children.

A related issue involves sharing a parent with stepsiblings. Not only do biological children have to share their parent with another adult, they also have to give up time with their parent to kids they barely know. Kids might wonder if Mom or Dad still loves them as much. They wonder if things will ever be like they were before.

This happened to a friend of mine who took in foster kids. When her daughter was a young teenager, the two of them were having a hard time finding things in common. Around that time, a foster daughter about the same age came to live with them. My friend and her foster daughter immediately connected and had a lot in common.

That's when my friend noticed a sudden change in her own daughter's mood. Her polite and easygoing girl became sassy and difficult. My friend was confused until I helped her see how the same emotions that are common to blended families came into the picture. Her biological daughter wasn't just jealous, she was afraid to lose her mother to this new "daughter."

Don't Be Harsh

Some remarried couples want peace so badly that they can demand too much too soon from the children. When kids act out of rebellion and disrespect in a blended family, there is often a lot of pain driving their actions and attitudes. Needless to say, stepfamilies require a lot of grace.

Blended-family parents should be quick to listen and slow to punish. Find out what's behind the behavior before you start doling out punishments. Don't silence kids. Let them speak. Most important, listen for what they're *not* saying. Dig for the fears behind their feelings.

My own son, Benjamin, is very logical. He wants to understand how and why each decision is made. If it makes sense to him, he can accept it. So he was already in a habit of asking "why" whenever I gave him an instruction. I knew his heart was (usually) in the right place, so I always tried to give him an answer.

But Robbie has a military background, so he believed that children asking "why" was evidence of disrespect. After we got married, Robbie would admonish my son for continuing a habit I always allowed, and in some ways, encouraged. I had to explain to my new husband Ben's desire to understand.

We agreed that Ben needed to have the right attitude and trust his parents. But Robbie, in turn, needed to have more grace and better accommodate Ben's specific personality traits.

When two households first come together, new norms haven't yet been established. What's typical in one house isn't typical in the other. So when the parents are too quick to change the rules, kids get confused. It's important for parents to discuss these troublesome areas before unilaterally establishing new rules.

I also recommend letting the kids know what you're thinking, especially if there are significant changes. Otherwise, how can you discipline them for breaking rules that you've never communicated?

Even after any new rules are communicated, you'll want to be patient with children as they process their questions or concerns. If children don't work through their emotions, tensions will only get worse. Let the children ask questions, even hard ones, and don't discipline them simply for asking questions that might seem harsh. Like my son, Ben, they need to process any changes and get answers to their questions.

Many kids, particularly younger ones, need a parent to help them put words to their feelings. You can say things like "You seemed bothered today when I spent time with your stepsister. Are you wondering if my feelings for you have changed? I want you to know that I couldn't possibly love her more than I already love you."

Sometimes when you ask children how they're doing, they simply say, "I'm fine." This is especially true for preteens and teenagers. They might not want to discuss or even admit their feelings. Or they may be concerned about offending you by admitting their frustrations.

Just keep in mind that for the first year or two (or four)—while everyone gets used to their new roles, schedules, and working through their emotions—perhaps your main role in the family is to help model grace for one another.

Ages and Stages

The ages of the children will make a difference in how your blended family functions. One of the hardest aspects of step-parenting is trying to figure out if your children are going through normal stages of maturity or if their current behavior is the result of blended-family dynamics.

I've compiled a few typical behaviors grouped by the children's ages. Our blended family has experienced some of these, but not all, so I'll share how they played out in our home.

You'll notice that I don't specifically include preschoolers in the following sections. That's not because preschoolers don't grieve. They do grieve in their own way. Authors John James and Russell Friedman suggest that children as young as eighteen months old can retain memories of close loved ones, so they are capable of experiencing the basic emotions of sadness and loss.[11]

But children this young typically grow out of their grief quickly. Most of their mental anguish is a response to a parent's grief and to changing circumstances.

I've noted that both my kids were babies when David died.

They definitely displayed signs of confusion and response to my sorrow, but it wasn't cognitive grief. They don't remember our life with him at all.

David's dad also died when David was a toddler. I once asked David about his memories of his father and whether he experienced grief. I asked him if he loved his dad. He said that he did, in a way. He said it was less like love and more like a bond. He likened it to the way we look at great-grandparents in photographs.

The biological parent essentially does the grieving for very young children. The child likely doesn't feel a profound sense of loss, but the parent feels it for the child.

Even though my kids didn't really grieve as babies, they do, however, remember the transition into remarriage. That's definitely true for Benjamin, who was five at the time. And they still struggle with the emotions that resulted from that transition.

A divorce during the first two years of a child's life can cause added grief for the custodial parent. A friend of mine recently went through a divorce. Even though her husband cheated on her multiple times, she tried to preserve their marriage for the sake of their two babies.

When it became clear that his cheating hadn't stopped, my friend accepted her need to get a divorce. But she couldn't stop worrying about how her children would suffer from not having their father in the same home. I told her that the kids would likely love the next man if she got remarried. "Yes," she said, "and that's what makes me sad."

Very young kids can experience a form of grief, but the real burden is carried by the parent.

Little Children

This is a category for kids aged four to nine. Children in this stage often have many misunderstandings about death, divorce, and remarriage. For example, little kids often get their perceptions of death from cartoons. Daffy Duck falls off a cliff and lives. Snow White merely needed a kiss to wake up. Movies end "happily ever after."

These depictions can be confusing to children, so we parents need to pay attention if we want to help little kids have a better understanding of reality. I was surprised, for example, to learn that some children think they caused the death of their parent or their parents' divorce.

Do you remember the story I told earlier about a young boy named Danny who was dying from cancer and the corresponding sadness of his best friend, Christopher? At Danny's eighth birthday party, Danny made a wish when he blew out the candles. Then he asked his friend, "Wanna know what I wished for?"

Danny wished to live to his ninth birthday.

But Danny didn't make it to his ninth birthday. Christopher became burdened that he'd caused his best friend's death because he didn't stop Danny from revealing his wish. "I always heard," he reasoned, "if you told anyone your wish, it wouldn't come true" (a line from the classic Disney movie *Cinderella*).[12]

That's how kids sometimes form their thinking about matters of life and death. They try to find an explanation—something that can answer the question "why"—and oftentimes they come up with no other explanation but to blame themselves.

Children might blame themselves when a parent leaves, concluding that if they were less fussy or better behaved, Mom or Dad wouldn't have left. They may think if they had only been a more loving child, the other parent would have stuck around.

It's important to take extra time with small children to help them understand what's going on with the people they love. They don't have to know all the gory details of a death, affair, or abuse. But they do need to know that it wasn't their fault.

Another common issue among younger kids is having unrealistic memories of a missing parent. They might remember their dad as the greatest person on earth, essentially akin to Superman. Or they may remember their mom as the most loving person who ever existed, much like an angel.

When Benjamin was much younger, for example, he would often fantasize that David was a much nicer daddy than Robbie, especially when Robbie did something Ben didn't like. Once he commented that David was the nicest of all his parents, and it was because he was shorter than me.

In reality, David was taller than me. And what did height have to do with being nice?

Turns out that Ben thought the order of authority in our

home was set by height. Since Robbie was the tallest, he was the boss, and since I was the next one in charge, he reasoned that I must have been taller than David. By his logic, since David was the shortest, he must have been the nicest. I don't know how Ben came to this conclusion, but that's how kids' imaginations work sometimes.

Another common reaction to trauma among young children is acting out. As I've said before, kids can't always understand their feelings, so their grief manifests in frustration. Acting out can also be a way to get attention if a child feels neglected or ignored.

I described that there's a tendency among many parents to excuse bad behavior in order to avoid dealing with it through boundaries and discipline. But not only will that hurt your children in the long run, it can also hurt your marriage.

Acknowledging your children's frustrations is not a justification for excusing their behavior. A better understanding, however, *will* help you in speaking with the children, showing empathy, and focusing on the root cause of their problems.

In seeking to understand, you can help your children communicate what they feel without fits of anger and frustration. No matter what kind of trauma kids have been through, they should still be expected to practice obedience and self-control.

The Bible has plenty to say about living self-controlled lives. One example is Titus 2:12, which tells us "to renounce ungodliness and worldly passions, and to live self-controlled, upright, and godly lives in the present age."

Achieving a measure of self-control will take time with children. As you deal with behavior problems, remember that peace is not the ultimate goal. Self-control is the goal. I say that because parents who focus too much on achieving peace will use distractions like television and other screens to help keep kids quiet. I made this mistake a lot as a single mom.

When my young children got hard to handle, I used the electronic nanny in my purse to occupy them instead of dealing with the issue. This tactic, however, came back to bite me when my son became addicted to games on my smartphone.

Ben was so attached to a screen that it literally changed his personality. I watched him become more aggressive, angry, and impatient. After several years of watching him struggle through almost daily fits of rage, I finally realized that the screen was the problem. It took a few weeks for him to calm down and return to a reasonable disposition after cutting off his smartphone access.

There's nothing wrong with a *healthy* diversion or distraction. Sometimes parents just need a break. But electronics were like a drug to my son. So try occupying your kids with activities that will add to their lives and not take away—activities like sports, dancing, art, music, writing, journaling, puzzles. There are all sorts of activities that don't involve screens.

Preteens and Teens

This section is for children aged ten to seventeen. This is the group that absorbs information everywhere they go. They are always listening, even when you think they aren't. That's why it's vital to tell them the truth. They ask the hard questions, and they want real answers.

Don't be like some of the parents Dr. Soder-Alderfer features in *With Those Who Grieve*. She shares the story of a couple whose son's best friend shot himself. The parents didn't want their boy to know that, so they told their son that his friend was cleaning a gun in the bathtub when he accidentally shot himself in the head. The explanation was ridiculous, and their son knew it.

The boy had to hear the truth from some mutual friends, and he was deeply hurt because he felt he should have heard the details of his best friend's death before everyone else knew. The two boys had been friends since early childhood.

"I just left [youth group] and cried all the way home," the young man recalled. "The next week my parents worried that I'd kill myself. I didn't want to kill myself. I just wanted someone to tell the truth about my friend."[13]

A vital part of grieving involves processing tough questions in our minds, but we can't truly process those questions until we know the truth.

Parents obviously need to break terrible news like this with empathy and sensitivity. It should never be delivered with a matter-of-fact attitude: "Oh, by the way, a person you deeply love won't be around anymore. Please pass the Parmesan."

Talking to kids about loss takes care and concern. It

requires your complete attention. They might need to ask questions for days. Let them.

Give them all the information you can, even if they don't fully understand it—even if you don't fully understand it. And let them know when you don't know all the answers. Sometimes not knowing feels better when you're not the only one.

Another typical response from kids in this stage is to shut down, fold into themselves, and search for identity. According to the counseling text *Dying and Grieving: Lifespan and Family Perspectives*, "Withdrawal may be related to a variety of beliefs, such as 'No one cares about me'; 'No one can possibly understand the emotional pain I am experiencing'; 'Others, too, may die and leave me, so it is wise not to get involved'; 'I am worthless and others will leave.'"[14]

Authors Alicia Skinner Cook and Kevin Ann Oltjenbruns explain that adolescents sometimes withdraw in order to keep from looking childish. Or, in sharp contrast, they might display overly strong emotions. As one fourteen-year-old said, "I just didn't know any way to let it out."[15]

This is where the biological parent needs to step in—to ask the hard questions and challenge the child's thinking. It's important that the biological parent does this because the bond between parent and child is long-established and difficult to break. Your teens or preteens know this bond is safe, that the biological parent will love them no matter what, so kids in this stage can push back *hard*. (This is also true of adolescents in general, whether or not they've experienced trauma.)

I like what I once heard at a parenting conference: Kids push back at parents the same way people push back on the safety bar of a roller coaster. They push on it hoping it will stay. They want to know for sure that it's safe and won't fail.

So do what's best for your kids, even if they dislike you for it. That means not spoiling them because you feel sorry for them. That means not letting them have the latest smartphone just because everyone else has it. That means not blindly accepting their suggestions. Kids need a parent to shepherd them, not a nursemaid to make them feel better.

It will likely take time, but a stepparent *can* become a "safe place" for teens and preteens. Some children are worried about saving face with their biological parent, but as a stepparent, you can be a non-judgmental party who offers advice and serves as a confidant.

When my teenage stepson told me about a crush or an embarrassing moment at school, I learned to keep those details from my husband because (I found out the hard way) Robbie would tease Seth about it. Seth talked to me about this stuff because he learned that I was trustworthy and wouldn't make fun of him.

Kids in this age group often seek out various coping mechanisms, such as substance abuse, sexual activity, and pornography. If these kinds of activities show up in your family, be sure to intervene with your child as soon as possible. Do whatever you can to keep the lines of communication open and seek professional help for your child if necessary.

Finally, like I said regarding younger kids, don't let your teens and preteens disappear into the land of screens. Keep them engaged in the real world. Find out what activities they enjoy and encourage their passions. Whether it's sports, dancing, art, or music, promote anything that occupies their minds that isn't limited to a screen.

Adult Children

People are often surprised when I bring up adult children while speaking about blended families. I've learned that adult children are sometimes more deeply affected by a remarriage than young children and teenagers.

For one thing, an adult child's grief process often takes longer. The family members still living at home have no way to avoid their grief or put it off. It's in their face every single day. Mostly because they have little choice in the matter, younger kids are typically able to work through their pain and start exploring new beginnings much sooner.

Adult children, however, often have a different dilemma— they want their parent to be happy, but at the same time, they have a hard time understanding how Mom or Dad could move on with life and love another.

When it comes to remarriage after death, many adult children want to believe their biological parents' love was so strong that even death couldn't break the bond they shared. That's why it's important to talk with adult children about what I emphasized in the beginning of this book: Mom or Dad can continue to love the deceased spouse deeply and still love another person. Those two loves aren't more or less, just different. They shouldn't be compared.

In the case of remarriage after a divorce, adult children might blame one parent or another. They may even become so angry that they refuse to speak to one or both parents. Please be patient with adult children who respond this way. Remember that anger is one of the steps in the grieving process. And working through emotional pain is necessary.

Much like younger children, some adult children of divorced parents continue to hope their parents will someday reunite. But when one or both parents remarry, that hope is dashed. The adult children might have been putting off their grief for years, longing for reconciliation. For them, the announcement of a remarriage is essentially the beginning of their grief.

You might also find that it's hard for your adult children to come back home. They have an entire childhood of memories with Mom or Dad, so a stepparent's mere presence is a tangible reminder of that loss.

That's why holidays can also be awkward. Adult children don't feel like they are coming *home*—they feel like they are intruding on a stranger's holiday. There are people from the other side of the family they don't even recognize. It's even awkward when a stepparent—a person they barely know—wants to be close to them. Adult stepchildren don't think of you as their stepmother or stepfather. They think of you as "Dad's wife" or "Mom's husband."

These situations might cause your adult children to distance themselves, which brings on yet another form of grief and loss for the biological parent.

From the outside looking in, it seems strange that adult children wouldn't be happy for their remarried parent who was able to find love again. But put yourself in their shoes. If both your parents are still alive, imagine if one of them died and the remaining parent remarried. (I'm guessing that's already happened with some of you reading this book.) How comfortable would you be around that new spouse? It would take some time, right? Well, they feel the same way.

If your adult stepchildren are willing to engage in a relationship, then begin by being a friend. Find things in common and bond over those topics, just like you would if you were meeting someone at church for the first time.

Don't feel obligated to talk about their other parent. At the same time, don't go out of your way to avoid the topic either. You can say something like "I bet it's strange to visit your father and see some strange woman in his house."

If they don't want to talk about it, that's okay too. If they do, then you've let them know that the subject isn't taboo. You're also letting them know you're available if they need a listening ear.

In short, don't expect adult stepchildren to immediately accept you into their lives. Some are able to do this, and I believe it is a special blessing when that happens. But many adult children struggle with the idea of a parent getting married again. Give them as much time and grace as you'd want them to give you.

Easing the Pressure

I've heard grief compared to a boiling tea kettle. Without a pressure valve, a boiling kettle would eventually explode. But if you allow some of the steam to leave the pot, the water can simmer without hurting anyone—and can also make a great cup of tea.

There might be a lot of pressure in your home right now, but it won't always be this way. Your family members might even reach a boiling point from time to time. That is a reality. Instead of trying to stifle them, give each member a chance to let off steam in a healthy way.

Authors John James and Russell Friedman write, "All loss is at 100 percent. There is no such thing as half grief. This is particularly true for children."[16] Adults might be tempted to believe that emotional pain isn't as difficult for kids. But they experience the same emotions that adults do.

By learning all you can about each child—past history, personality traits, talents, and interests—you can help guide them through their emotional journey and bring something beautiful out of it.

After all, God is in the healing and redemption business.

HOME FOR
THE HOLIDAYS

THERE ARE DAYS WHEN EMOTIONS pour down on you like rain. You weren't expecting it, then you hear that song on the radio that reminds you of a particular memory. You might spot someone with a familiar profile. You might smell a fragrance that the person you loved used to wear.

Popular women's author Lois Rabey described the power of her late husband's cologne: "I'd sometimes sprinkle drops of Royal Copenhagen from his half-used bottle onto my pillowcase. I'd bury my head in the pillow and inhale deeply. And then I'd cry for a long time."[1]

Then there are days when the absence of a loved one is palpable—the anniversary of a death, the wedding anniversary of a deceased spouse, the person's birthday, even Mother's or Father's Day. These special dates can be brutal.

The days leading up to the date might be calm, or they might be stressful. We might not even understand why we're emotional or more on edge than usual. It's as if our hearts know but our minds haven't caught up yet.

I remember times when I wrung my hands for weeks, dreading the approach of my wedding anniversary or the anniversary of David's death. But when the day finally arrived, it was never as bad as I anticipated. And that brought a sigh of relief—until I realized that *not* being sad was also kind of sad.

There were times when I forgot about a certain anniversary, and it was already nighttime before I realized the day had passed. That's the worst kind of sad, at least for me. It was sad because I forgot, which meant the date didn't mean as much to me as it used to, even though it really did.

I'll never forget the first Christmas after David died. I dreaded the sadness I would feel on Christmas Day because I thought it would be painfully obvious that he wasn't there. I spent the entire week before Christmas mentally preparing myself to have the worst Christmas of my life.

But then Christmas came, and it was beautiful. I wasn't sad at all. Having family around who missed him as much as I did was comforting. I couldn't believe how much emotional energy I expended "getting ready" for Christmas.

Emotions never show up quite when or how you think they will. Thanks to having holidays sprinkled throughout the year, hardly a month goes by when there isn't something on the calendar that sends a flash of pain through our hearts. Then we're compelled to ride the emotional roller coaster once again.

It's nearly impossible to predict the cycle, but at least you can prepare yourself to expect that holidays and other special days will include an element of grief, and you can accept that this cycle could go on for years. It might impact the holidays for the rest of your life.

In this chapter, I hope to give you some idea of what to expect and how to respond to the challenges of blended-family holidays and events—and to also help you enjoy these special days!

A Word of Caution

Before I get into the practical part of this chapter, I want to issue a word of warning to all parents, but especially to stepmothers. When a tenderhearted parent hears that certain days create sorrow in a child's heart, most will want to do something to help that child work through the pain.

Such a parent has only the child's best interests at heart. I know that, and you know that. Yet if you step too far into a child's emotions and try to force the healing process, it can seem like a passive-aggressive way of taking over for the missing parent, like you are trying to exert dominance.

And what was originally done with kind and pure motivations can actually push a stepchild further away.

I've read other books by stepparenting authorities who

have never experienced the personal loss of an intimate family member, and often they advise new stepparents to create ceremonies, write letters, or implement other forms of therapy that are meant to help the family heal. As someone who has gone through such a loss, I would advise against having a stepparent coordinate these sorts of activities or events.

They might be a good exercise for a therapist or a biological family member to coordinate, but for a *stepparent*—even with the best intentions—to lead the family in such activities comes across as sticking one's nose where it doesn't belong.

One story I heard was particularly painful. The stepmother decided that the family needed a "good-bye" ceremony to help give them closure. She arranged everything for the ceremony, set the time and place, then told the family about it.

She thought they would be delighted, but—to her surprise—the kids didn't want to do it. So she talked to her husband about it, and he agreed with the kids. He said if the kids didn't want to do it, they should all respect that and call it off. It was *their* mother, after all.

That's when this stepmother should have dropped the whole issue and moved on, reminding herself to avoid putting all that effort into something without checking first. But no, she decided to proceed with the ceremony anyway.

Without the rest of the family.

Yes, you read that right. I cringed when I heard that story. She didn't even know the deceased woman. I realize that she felt a certain bond with her because they shared children. But as a person who has lost a spouse, this grated on me.

If the kids and her husband had *invited* her to do something like this, it would have been okay. But because she took it upon herself, it was awkward and insulting. I don't know any of these family members, yet I still feel like the kids were violated. Honoring a deceased loved one is an intensely personal matter.

However you decide to handle anniversaries and other special days, just make sure you follow the lead of your stepfamily members. Be sensitive, don't take the lead, and extend as much grace as you possibly can.

If your family members aren't in the mood to commemorate the person or the day, then don't make them. Your goal is more about *recognizing* their emotions than about forcing them to work through those feelings.

Space for Memorial

When handling holidays and special days, keep in mind that feelings are personal and individual. Every member of your blended family will have a different response to particularly poignant dates on the calendar.

Unfortunately, since emotions are messy and don't operate in a predictable straight line, it's impossible to prepare for every possible reaction. Thankfully, you don't have to.

So what should you do for your blended family when you

know they are coming up on one of those special anniversaries? Honestly, nothing. Not unless they suggest it.

You don't need to help your family remember a special anniversary. If they want to remember it, great. If they want to forget it, that's fine too. If you want to help, offer a place and a time for memorials to take place. Make room in your life for it. But be sure to speak with your spouse about it. If he or she doesn't think it's a good idea, then don't get involved! The biological family might not want to share that day with you, and that's okay.

Don't be offended if they don't need your help. In *With Those Who Grieve*, Kay Soder-Alderfer writes, "The person is not rejecting you or your ability to give; he or she is just saying, 'I need to grieve my own way—including the help I accept.'"[2]

Soder-Alderfer has a list of practical guidelines for when others are grieving:[3]

1. Accept that moods will change drastically. People in grief don't act "normal."
2. Don't think you can fix the situation. You can't.
3. If you are a "doer," then don't overdo. Let the grieving persons choose what they do and do not need.
4. Give a hug. Lend an ear. Allow space.
5. Validate the grief.
6. Talk about the good you see in the life of the person they lost.

7. Be sincere. If you didn't know the deceased person, don't act like you did. Instead talk about what you do know.
8. Say the name of the person they lost. Don't avoid it.
9. Don't give advice unless you are asked for it.
10. Pray for the griever.
11. Be ready to learn.
12. Don't follow these guidelines like strict rules. Use your common sense.

I would also suggest that, if the parent is deceased, there be a place where the kids can go to honor their deceased parent. My children and I can visit David's grave, but Kari was cremated, and Robbie hasn't found the right place and time to spread her ashes. Instead, Robbie and his sons go to Disney World to remember and connect with her, because that was her favorite place in the world.

I'm not suggesting that there has to be a gravesite visit in order to spend time thinking about a loved one. I do believe, however, that a resting place can help give closure to the grievers. At least to me, it provides a finality and completeness to mourn in the place where the body (or ashes) is laid.

That's one of the saddest parts, I think, about remarriage after a divorce. I've heard people tell me, "At least you can mourn the loss of your spouse. I'm not allowed to mourn because I'm divorced." I'm sure many kids feel the same way. Their parent isn't dead, after all, yet there is still reason to mourn.

Probably the best thing you can do when those special days are approaching is to be open to suggestions. You can even make some suggestions if you want. Nothing *has* to be planned. Nothing *has* to be done. But at least let it be known that it is always allowed.

Anniversaries

To avoid being caught off guard by potential reminders of sadness and hurt, discuss what those days are and when they occur. Begin with the most obvious days—anniversaries. There are all kinds of anniversaries to know about. Here are a few in our house:

- Robbie and Kari's wedding anniversary (January)
- Kari's birthday (July)
- The day Kari died (July)
- David and Sabrina's wedding anniversary (September)
- David's birthday (March)
- The day David died (September)

For couples remarried after divorce, there are going to be other days that have special significance. Maybe the wedding date of a previous marriage or the date a divorce was finalized.

You might be confused why these days should cause sadness, especially if your current marriage is healthier than the previous one. It's because any marriage is a special kind of relationship, and you will always feel connected to that person in one way or another. It's an aspect of grief that you might live with for the rest of your life, and that's okay.

It's good to know when these days are coming. You can't do anything to prevent them, but at least you can know why family members might seem melancholy, distant, or grumpier than usual. You might want to note these dates on your calendar, like I have. Marking the dates help me know when I might need to have a little more grace.

Special Places

Dates on a calendar aren't the only emotional triggers. Special places can also create strong emotions. Familiar sights and smells can transport you back in time. It sometimes feels like you're there again with the one you loved, only that person is no longer around.

Being in some places without that other person doesn't feel right. The loss can seem egregious in those moments. All you really want is to wander in the nostalgia, accessing only the positive memories—the moments of laughter and love—that remain stored in the deep recesses of your mind.

Our senses are a powerful memory-retrieval system. Events that we haven't thought about for years can come flooding back when triggered by a certain taste, smell, or sound.

But now you're here with another spouse or another parent. And that person doesn't share those same memories. So once again, you (or your spouse, or your children) feel the need to take the grief inward.

Here are some of the special places that prompt a lot of remembering in our family:

- Destin, Florida—a favorite vacation place for both Kari and David
- Disney World—Kari's favorite place on earth
- San Antonio, Texas—Kari and Robbie's honeymoon destination
- Hot Springs, Arkansas—the location of David's death

Destin, Florida, was where I learned how special places can have such a strong connection. David and I took a weeklong vacation to Destin every year. We even spent our first anniversary there. When he died I continued the tradition and went there with groups of friends.

When Robbie and I got married, I naturally planned for us the same vacation that I did every year. I didn't realize at the time that I scheduled our trip the same week as the anniversary of Kari's death. I thought the laid-back ocean atmosphere would relax Robbie and Seth and help them deal with some of their sorrow.

I also didn't know at the time that Destin was one of Kari's favorite places. Their family vacationed there numerous times before she was diagnosed with skin cancer.

I didn't know about any of this, but I did notice Robbie was more easily upset than usual during that trip—and it was more than the normal anniversary sensitivity. He seemed to turn inward and cared little about what was going on with anyone but himself.

Of course, the reason I didn't know about the location's special meaning to Kari was because Robbie went inward and didn't tell me.

He hadn't been to Destin since the last time he'd visited with Kari. Just being in Destin was bringing up painful feelings and memories—the smells and sounds of the ocean and the feeling of wet sand between his toes.

We still visit there almost every year. After all, it's a place with special memories for all of us. But now we schedule our trip for a different week. And even though I can't change the emotions that Robbie feels at the beach, I'm at least aware that he might seem more standoffish or sensitive. So I set my expectations accordingly to allow room for sorrow.

My mother keeps suggesting that I take my kids to Disney World. She says every kid needs to go. But I just can't bring myself to do it. Kari loved the place so much that it's become a symbol of her family's love and bonding. Both of Robbie's sons even went to Disney World for their honeymoons.

Maybe I'm wrong, but I feel like taking my kids to Disney World would be akin to stomping on Kari's grave. And can you imagine what the sights and smells might do to Robbie? I suspect it would *not* be the happiest place on earth, nor a fun-filled trip for the whole family!

Mother's Day and Father's Day

Other potentially awkward dates for blended families are Mother's Day and Father's Day. For children who already miss their biological parent terribly, these two holidays are yet more salt in those wounds.

During the weeks leading up to these holidays, every advertisement, billboard, church program, and school event—not to mention social media—turns into a blinking, blaring reminder that either Mom and Dad are split up or one of them is gone. (Thanks for the tears, Hallmark!)

When Mother's Day comes around, I'm ready to celebrate, but my poor husband is ready to crawl into a hole and wish it all away. Not only does he face the loss of his children's mother, he also faces the untimely loss of his own mother. Somehow, he always finds an excuse to go fishing or hunting on that day every year. The new spouse has to navigate a tricky situation.

Let me explain. First, I am a mother, but I'm not the mother of Robbie's sons. On Mother's Day I expect Robbie to help my kids celebrate my contribution to their lives. But this is hard for him. Even though he wants to help celebrate me, it's difficult for him to put on a happy face on such a sad day.

Second, I'm also a stepmother. I'm not the mother of Robbie's children, but when Seth lived with us, I filled the role of a mother. Though I could never take the place of his mom, I still had plenty of jobs to do for him. Yet on Mother's

Day, I wasn't the object of his affections. His real mother was. If anything, my being there was a harsh reminder that she no longer was. That's hard for a kid to understand!

Stepmoms in particular can take Mother's Day very hard. They handle the duties of a mother but don't seem to qualify for the celebration. They make lunches, keep up with school-work, talk to teachers, play taxi driver, maintain schedules, receive complaints, watch out for emotional distress, and generally keep the entire family on the same page.

It's true that blended-family members should be generous and celebrate all the parents. That would be ideal, but in emotionally charged circumstances it's hard for anyone to be generous. And maybe stepparents shouldn't be so sensitive. But again, especially in emotionally charged circumstances, it's hard to be the bigger person and not feel passed over.

So blended families usually end up stumbling through the day, either awkwardly avoiding the elephant in the room or offering trite gestures out of obligation. That's partly because there isn't an established social protocol for how to celebrate Mother's Day or Father's Day within a blended family. Add in the issue of unmet expectations and the whole thing can turn into an emotional mess.

So . . . how do you manage this awkward time?

First, talk to your spouse *before* the holiday. Sometimes a spouse simply doesn't realize how you feel. Do you want to be acknowledged? What are your expectations? Sometimes a basic conversation is enough to help straighten everything out.

Second, consider lowering your expectations. Stepparents should realize that their spouse is caught between a rock and a hard place to a degree. If he or she acknowledges you on this special holiday, the kids might be offended that their biological mom or dad wasn't honored even more, or perhaps not treated special *enough*.

Kids tend to evaluate how a stepparent is treated compared to the biological parent. That's when you hear things like "You never did that for Mom!" Gifts, messages of thanks, special attention—it's all susceptible to judgment, whether it is good enough or too good, and what your motives are. Biological parents dread the emotional torture of such comparisons.

The good news is that you—the stepparent—have the ability to remove all the drama from this kind of reaction. You can do that by lowering your expectations. Accept the fact that this holiday is not yours alone. Let the biological parent enjoy the holiday with his or her biological kids.

Many blended families address this issue by setting aside a different day to celebrate the stepparent. It doesn't have to be a holiday—any day will do. Pick a day and declare it as Stepparent's Day! And it doesn't have to be a major celebration. Just a bouquet of flowers or movie tickets, some treats, and a sweet note. That's all it takes.

Third, if you have your own biological children, help them celebrate you. As I mentioned already, Robbie has a hard time celebrating me on Mother's Day. I'm not his mother and I'm not the mother of his children. He tries to leave town on that day every year.

At first, it hurt my feelings because I expected to be treated a certain way. I love being a mom and wanted to be celebrated for it. But when I view things from Robbie's perspective, I honestly understand.

One year I decided to let it go and stop pressuring him to do something he really didn't feel like doing. Yes, it let him off the hook, but it also let me off the hook. I didn't have to be angry anymore or feel sorry for myself all week leading up to that day. It allowed me to focus on celebrating my own children and letting them celebrate me.

I usually tell my kids to make me a card or sing me songs or whatever else I think of at the time. They love giving me what I ask for, and I love getting it! They don't take me out to eat or buy me gifts, but I really don't need anything. The love they give in their childish ways is enough to last a lifetime— and it fits better in a scrapbook!

The Most Wonderful Time of the Year

"There's no place like home for the holidays!" Except when a parent dies or a family splits, in which case there's nowhere *worse* to be than home for the holidays.

One year Robbie's oldest son, Will, and his wife were driving in from Dallas to stay a few days at our house for Christmas. Even though Robbie and I had been married for a while, this was their first visit during the holidays. I knew it might be hard for them.

I did my best to make our house a warm, welcoming place, but there was no way to make it feel like the home of Will's childhood. Even if I were somehow able to magically recreate the atmosphere of the past, my presence alone was a reminder that both the home and the person Will remembered were gone. No matter what, that reality cannot be disguised or replaced.

After a great loss, family holidays are forever changed. That's just the way it is. It's not fair. It's hard. And sometimes, it just plain stinks. But God never said life would be easy. And I'm actually glad that life's not fair. I'm glad God treats me "unfairly" because He treats me with grace that I don't deserve.

And that's the way we should treat each other—with grace. Especially on those special occasions when traditions and expectations collide. Even though things are different in a blended family, these days can still be celebrated and enjoyed. Here are a few things I've learned about Thanksgiving and Christmas.

Embrace the sorrow. Don't try to smooth over conflicting emotions. Acknowledge them. Don't let sorrow be the elephant in the room. Say, "Gosh, I know you must be thinking about your mom/dad. What is one of your favorite memories or traditions about Christmas?"

Talk to your stepchildren about their feelings. Listen to their stories and ask questions. These conversations involve sharing sadness at Christmas, but they also involve sharing love.

Embrace traditions and customs from both sides of the family. Philippians 2:3-4 says, "In humility count others more significant than yourselves. Let each of you look not only to his own interests, but also to the interests of others." Blended families might start out looking like the opposing teams of a football game—each family has a different coaching style and a different set of plays based on years of competing together. The best way to become a united team is to pause the game, give up the desire to compete, and learn to work from the same playbook.

To love my husband and stepchildren with the love of Christ means I can't just disregard their family history. I need to embrace parts of it as my own. For example, before our first Christmas together, Robbie and I discussed the traditions his boys were used to. What were their expectations? What holiday foods did they like? Did they receive certain gifts or treats in their stockings? Did they open gifts on Christmas Eve or only on Christmas morning?

I also talked to Seth. I wanted to know what he wanted or expected during the holidays. And I made sure that his grandparents were welcome and included in all our holiday celebrations. A little research goes a long way.

I didn't try to recreate Kari's home or take her place. God established a new home with our marriage. But I did want to build our new foundation with bits and pieces of what we all brought from our pasts. I certainly never expected Robbie or his sons to abandon their past in order to accommodate me and my kids.

In the end, I used decorations from both homes, played movies that both families enjoyed, and made foods and treats based on everyone's requests. I also included a few holiday surprises—perhaps the beginning of some new traditions.

Why not start creating your own holiday traditions—some special things that only your blended family does together? This is particularly fun when both spouses have children from previous marriages.

It can be hard to get the whole group together for Thanksgiving or Christmas, but if you make your own traditions, the kids have something to look forward to at your house with the whole blended family. This might mean a family game night, Nerf gun wars, a cookie-baking day—there are hundreds of ideas that you can come up with or find online. The idea is to make these new traditions fun for everyone—something the kids *like*, not just something you *want* them to like. And try to do them on a day when everyone can be there.

Also, take *lots* of pictures and share them with the kids! When they look back on the photos, they will remember how much fun they had and look forward to these moments every year.

Center Thanksgiving and Christmas around their true meanings. Family-centered traditions are wonderful, but they aren't the most important part of the holidays.

Somewhere along the way, the holidays became about creating perfect experiences, and maybe that's why they're so hard on blended families. Brokenness, after all, is definitely not perfect. That's why it's important to remember what Thanksgiving and Christmas are really about: giving thanks and celebrating the birth of our Savior—the One who was perfect so that we don't have to be.

We can take all our sorrows and griefs to Jesus, and we can thank the Lord that a time is coming when there will be no more pain and no more tears (see Revelation 21:4). While we're on this earth we can forgive and forget, we can love even when we're not loved, and we can bear one another's burdens, just as He did for us. And our blended families can be a testament to the very reason why we celebrate.

HANDLING REJECTION: WHEN KIDS DON'T WANT TO BLEND

LOTS OF BLENDED-FAMILY WEDDINGS have a "blending of the sands" ceremony. This is when family members from each side of the blended family come to the altar and each individual pours different colored sand into the same glass container. The result is a multicolored work of art that symbolizes the various lives coming together as one family.

It's a beautiful sentiment, but does it really reflect reality in a blended family? Speaking metaphorically, what if one person doesn't want to pour all their sand into the glass container? What if someone doesn't want to pour any? What if the glass container reflected a more realistic depiction of your stepfamily, and it looked less like a work of art and more like a jar partially filled with the leftover dust from a chalkboard?

Blended-family expert Ron Deal tackles this issue by demonstrating how the container might look if the sands were combined in the way that stepfamily members blend their families in the real world.[1]

Deal begins with two vials of sand that represent the new husband and wife. He completely empties both vials of sand into the glass container. This signifies that husband and wife are both all-in and ready to blend. The youngest child's sand is poured in next, and it goes in all the way.

When Deal gets to the older children—some his, some hers—things become less consistent. Barely half the sand from some vials makes it into the container. Other vials offer just a sprinkle. At one point, he puts a divider in the container and only pours sand in on one side. One child pours all his sand into the glass container, changes his mind, and scoops most of it out again.

The first time I witnessed this demonstration, I thought, *Now we're getting to reality!* I couldn't wait for Deal's conclusion so that I could hear his best solutions for this messy display.

When Deal was done, he said something like "See that? It's not pretty. It's messy." Okay, I was with him so far. Then he said, "But it's okay. You need to learn to live with it."

I did not like that at all. Learn to live with *messy*? That's hard! How can we have a *blended* family if everyone doesn't pour in completely?

Deal's point is that we can't always have things the way we want them, and there's basically nothing we can do about it. So instead of spinning our wheels and trying to create the so-called perfect family, we're better off accepting reality, giving the situation some time, and focusing on the ones who are really pouring into the family. The others should be covered in prayer.

By definition, blended families are created out of brokenness, and with brokenness comes imperfection. If we want to maintain fruitful, fulfilling lives, we have to live like the little wildflowers that pop up between cracks in the sidewalk. Those flowers soak up the rain, reach deep into the soil, and grow toward the sun, even if the elements they need to grow are difficult to attain.

We, too, can embrace the elements we've been given in our less-than-ideal circumstances. Like the brightly colored petals of the wildflowers, we can thrive under God's care—no matter how imperfectly our sand is blended.

Not for the Fainthearted

This doesn't mean there's little hope for blending *your* family. Maybe those who haven't poured their sand all the way in just aren't ready yet. The time might come when they change their minds—but until then, don't despair.

Remember that in biological families, relationships form more organically. But in blended families it takes time and diligence, requiring forgiveness, understanding, and the willingness to work through the uncomfortable moments.

Most of us have a natural tendency to avoid awkward situations, and that means withdrawing, leaving the room, or remaining silent and guarded during a conversation. But when blended families behave this way toward each other, it usually comes across as cold, rude, and spiteful.

That's rarely the intention of most family members, even the unhappy ones. It's just the typical ebb and flow of awkward blended-family life.

Ecclesiastes 3:1-8 offers a beautiful explanation of this natural ebb and flow, and the passage is particularly powerful when considered in the context of remarriage. The various seasons described involve both letting go of the past and embracing new blessings. Here are just a few:

- a time to tear down and a time to build up
- a time to cry and a time to laugh
- a time to grieve and a time to dance
- a time to search and a time to quit searching
- a time to keep and a time to throw away (NLT)

Time is the key ingredient when blending two families. Like letting dough rise, there's really no way to rush it. This time of waiting allows us—actually compels us—to experience both sides of these scriptural seasons, and the hard work pays off as God promises: He makes "everything beautiful in its time" (Ecclesiastes 3:11).

Feeling Betrayed

It's almost always easier for a person outside a situation to see the beauty in it. For example, it's one thing to take a helicopter ride above the Grand Canyon, awed by the colors and the grandeur. It's quite another to be lost in the depths of the same canyon, alone and without water, not knowing if you will make it out alive. It's the same Grand Canyon, yet from two vastly different perspectives.

So what do you do when you're a stepparent wandering in the Grand Canyon of blended-family rejection? You're lost, you're hurting, and you don't know what to do.

It's especially difficult when you're a stepparent who's gone all-in with your blended family, opening up, pouring out, being vulnerable, and making sacrifices. Yet even as you fully commit to this alliance with the other family members, you get stabbed in the back.

It feels like a made-for-television movie: *Grand Canyon: Mafia-Style*.

You, the new stepparent, originally viewed yourself as a means to help fill the gaps caused by death or divorce in the lives of your stepchildren. But your desire to help is exactly what so many stepchildren are afraid of. They don't want that! The competing agendas draw a line in the sand, putting the new family members on opposite sides.

It feels like you can't make anyone happy. No matter what you say, you're seen as the enemy. No matter what you do, it's viewed as an attack. In the minds of your adversaries, the only way to get rid of the threat is to defeat the enemy.

While you are attempting to broker peace, other family members are showering you with arrows of insults, setting verbal traps, and quietly gassing you with rolling eyes and bad attitudes.

It makes you feel foolish and disenchanted. You might even begin to regret your decision to marry into this family. You realize that while you were ready to give everything to make this blended family work, some other family members see you as an adversary.

But since you're not a quitter, the best course of action is to be patient and empathetic—try to see things from their perspective. Demonstrate grace for others, even when they are unkind to you. Keep the lines of communication open with everyone in your home and allow them to air their grievances.

I know that's not always easy. In fact, it can be quite difficult. It's tough to be subjective, kind, and rational when you're the target of constant ridicule, always on guard for another surprise attack. How do you sort things out rationally when you're worried about stepping on a land mine and accidently detonating the whole family?

You might be tempted to set traps of your own. You might even pull out a verbal machine gun and start blasting accusations at everyone and everything in your way.

Yet in the aftermath of such a rampage, you witness the damage your outburst caused to the relationships, the trust, and the already fragile foundation of your struggling blended family. Guilt quickly floods in, and you once again feel like you're drowning in your own regrets.

That's the moment when you attempt an immediate reversal. You try anything to make the resistant family members like you, but it's yet another mistake. The attempt misfires badly because it makes them recoil even more.

Stop.

Stop trying to *make* anyone like you. Instead, just be you. You can't control what others do, what others feel, what others think. It's up to them to help make the blended-family relationship work. It's their choice whether they pour their sand into the container.

When you make a genuine mistake, tell the others you're sorry, ask for their forgiveness, then move on. Whether they decide to work with you or against you is between them and God.

Widowed author Judith Fabisch writes, "Christ died so we could be free of our burden of guilt."[2] Your heart can be freed from guilt, but you can't change another person's heart. That's a job for the Holy Spirit.

Many people prefer to push others away rather than put in the effort to forge new relationships. Sometimes family members are actively looking for mistakes, just so they have an excuse not to like you. And if they look hard enough for mistakes, they're eventually going to find them. You're only human, after all, and we all make mistakes.

When Forced to Choose

Feeling betrayed and battle weary can make an otherwise healthy person turn on his or her new spouse. The inner questions quickly pile up:

- *Why doesn't my spouse keep these attacks from happening?*
- *Why didn't he help me out more and take my side for once?*
- *How could she let the children treat me this way?*
- *Doesn't he understand and empathize with what I'm going through?*
- *Does she really love me if she keeps letting this happen?*

Stepparents can be so overwhelmed by the pain and rejection that we fail to see how these same situations also hurt the biological parent. No one wants to see their own children—their flesh and blood—reject the person they now love.

When kids refuse to blend in a blended family—when they refuse to even try—the biological parent feels forced to choose between a relationship with the kids or with the spouse. And that's a tough position to be in!

Biological parents are often more surprised than the new stepparent when the kids are not cooperative. After all, a parent usually marries someone they think is a good fit for the family. I don't know of anyone who said, "You know, my family is going to hate this person, but I'm going to marry him/her anyway." For parents who genuinely love their children, that's ridiculous!

During the dating phase, many parents go so far as to get their children on board with the relationship, even seeking their approval of the person they want to marry. These parents know that their children's lives will be affected by whomever they marry, so they want to know that their children feel comfortable with the fit.

But even when children give their approval for their parent's new love interest, those same children often end up disgruntled and uncooperative after the marriage. That's because most kids aren't mature enough to realize that they probably won't feel the same way about the person once they all start living in the same home.

It's normal to become annoyed with the quirky habits of the new person in the family, or to feel frustrated by changes to the old routine. Even the adults feel this tension in the first years of married life, so of course the kids will feel it too. That's all part of the adjustment period in a blended family.

But when the biological parents start feeling sorry for their children, they often begin to blame themselves for all sorts of issues. Biological parents might feel bad about mistakes they made during the single-parenting years. And now they might feel bad about remarrying and disrupting family life.

Biological parents aren't sure what to do when they feel caught between their spouse and their kids. They love them all, and they don't want to choose. They worry that if they choose their spouse over their kids, they might alienate their kids forever. That's a daunting choice to face.

They might try to straddle the fence and support both sides at the same time. Or they'll remain in the middle and try to be a peacemaker. Either way, they end up taking fire from both camps.

Some biological parents try to stake out a neutral position or even pretend that the conflict isn't happening—trying to convince their spouse that everything is a big misunderstanding or the result of an overactive imagination. Of course, this never works. More likely, it only adds to the feelings of bitterness in the family and creates a longer period of unrest, which prevents healing. Supporting each other as husband and wife is actually the most stable and loving choice you can make for the entire family.

I'm not giving you this perspective to use as a weapon or to help you fortify your position in the marriage. I'm giving you this information because I want you to have empathy—to feel some of the same pain that your spouse feels when put in a position where he or she is forced to choose. You need to understand the difficulty of this position.

If you are the biological parent who has been forced to choose, I challenge you to take a hard look in the mirror. Are you leaving your spouse to fend for himself or herself in a conflict with your children? Do you treat your spouse the way you would want to be treated in the same situation? Have you put your fears of upsetting your children over the covenantal promises you made to your spouse in the sight of God?

Dealing with uncooperative children isn't easy for anyone, but sacrificing your spouse is a choice you should never have to make.

What's a Stepparent to Do?

It's good to have an intellectual understanding of blended-family concerns, but I'm a practical person. I want to know what to *do* when I'm faced with the tough issues.

I've learned that you don't have to let others run over you. There are practical actions you can take when you feel like an outsider in your own home. I've compiled a list of several ideas that have helped me, not just with issues of blending, but with all kinds of problems in life.

Allow yourself to hurt. No one comes into a blended family hoping that their stepchildren will reject them. We all dream that everyone will get along, or at least enjoy each other's company. When that doesn't happen, there is hurt, and where there is hurt, there is a need to grieve. So let yourself feel sad.

But don't lose hope. Things *can* change and often do, especially as the children get older. Sometimes a change of heart requires several years of maturity.

I know a woman named Susan, now in her seventies, who spent several decades as a stepmother. She said her adult stepchildren hated her at first, and her husband had a hard time recognizing the rejection she experienced.

But the longer they were married, the more those adult children got used to Susan. It wasn't easy and it took many years, but they finally reached the point where they were all comfortable being together. Now they can laugh at their tumultuous early years as a family.

You might look at the trajectory of your blended family and think you know what the future holds. Maybe that future looks bleak, but it is not written in stone. God is in the business of changing hearts, and He can still work wonders.

Take a breather. Step away from tense situations. Go outside and take a deep breath. Talk to your spouse before you talk to your stepchildren. Listen more than you speak.

This is perhaps my greatest weakness as a stepmother. I typically wait until I'm just about to explode before I open my mouth. And then, well, I explode. I've ruminated about the issue so much that by the time I start speaking, my opponents can't think of a single argument that I haven't already had with them in my head.

Needless to say, that approach never, ever, ever, ever goes over well. I've burned a few bridges in my history as a stepmother, and it's mainly because I let the hurt, anger, or whatever build up too much. And when the conflict begins, I'm ready to fight, not listen.

Always show love—even when it's not returned. Jesus says in Matthew 5:44, "Love your enemies and pray for those who persecute you." One of the hardest actions is to love someone who consistently disrespects you or ignores your gestures of kindness. That's why we need the Holy Spirit in us—to give us this supernatural ability!

What helped me was to consider Kari. When I got really irritated with my teenage stepson and felt bitterness setting in, I would ask myself, *If Kari were in my place and I in hers, what would I want her to do for my children?*

That question reminded me that my stepson had suffered the loss of his mother. If my children lost me, I would want a woman in their lives who would give them as much grace as possible and who would work hard to be a friend, not an enemy.

Stepparents have lots of opportunities to practice living a life directed by God's Spirit. There are certainly days when this is harder than others, and on those days, pray. Think about your family in the future and consider the love you are giving them now—even if it feels like there is no return on your emotional investment. Hold on to hope that someday it *will* pay off.

Pray, pray, pray. I probably don't have to remind you to pray. Prayer should be standard equipment in a stepparent's spiritual toolbox. But I do want to remind you that God is in control of your blended family.

You can't change the members of your family, and you certainly can't make them do what you want them to. But you can appeal to the One who is able to change hearts and minds. Philippians 4:6-7 says,

> Do not be anxious about anything, but in everything
> by prayer and supplication with thanksgiving let
> your requests be made known to God. And the peace
> of God, which surpasses all understanding, will
> guard your hearts and your minds in Christ Jesus.

There is too much to handle on your own in a blended family. The good news is you don't have to, even if your spouse isn't always supportive. There will be times when you need to step away from the situation and pray, *God, this is a matter of the heart. I have to leave this one up to You.*

Don't give up! Remarriages don't exactly have a reputation for their endurance. That's no wonder considering the unexpected frustrations and pressures. Many are caught off guard by the sheer number and variety of issues they have to work through.

That's why some people simply stop trying. They feel guilty and convince themselves that they made a mistake. But God has demonstrated time and again that He can bring beauty from ashes. He can turn mourning into gladness (see Isaiah 61:3). If He can do all the wonders we see in Scripture, then He can form a family out of two broken homes. Don't give up.

What about When I Lose It?

I'm willing to admit that I've blown my top more than a few times during our years as a blended family. Stepfamilies are hard. They're emotional. They can test the fabric of your humanity. And sometimes one of those threads in the fabric snaps.

But you haven't committed some unforgivable sin, even if your stepchildren or your spouse make you feel that way. Yes, actions have consequences, but actions can also be forgiven.

So, the first thing you need to do is apologize. You need to do this even if they don't forgive you. You should do it even if everything blows over. You should do it simply because it's the right thing to do.

Next, if it's a child you snapped at, have the biological parent speak to them. Your spouse should come to your defense and help the others see things from your perspective.

This isn't to excuse your behavior. Blowing your top was wrong. But if the kids can understand how and why it happened, it might help them forgive you and maybe avoid another blowup in the future.

Early in our marriage, Robbie blew up at Benjamin. There were still a lot of hurt feelings the next day, even after Robbie apologized. When I talked to Ben about it, I said, "Ben, when you do something wrong or lose control of your emotions, don't you want people to forgive you?"

"Yes," he said.

"Then do you think you can forgive Daddy?"

Putting the shoe on the other foot seemed to connect in his young mind, and he was willing to forgive after that.

On another occasion, Ben was ranting about getting in trouble for hitting his sister. He thought Robbie had been too harsh.

"Dad is not your enemy," I explained. "He doesn't discipline you to hurt you or threaten you. He's teaching you that violence is wrong. You will be a man someday, and violence as a man is a lot harsher than it is as a boy. Learn that lesson now."

The next day, not only was Ben over the incident, but it also seemed to bring him closer to his stepdad.

The truth is that this conflict resolved easier than most. Things usually don't work out so well. Sometimes, even when you ask for forgiveness, others in your blended family will use your mistake against you in the future. Even if you think the issue is over and forgiven, stepchildren will bring up a past hurt months or even years later.

Just the other day my son brought up an incident that had hurt his feelings more than seven years ago. I didn't even know he remembered it! And out of nowhere, he used it to lob an emotional bomb at his stepfather.

Finally, receive God's forgiveness for yourself and resolve to keep working on your self-control. You can't dictate the feelings of your family members. They *should* forgive you as they have been forgiven, but it might take a while for them to realize that. Maybe years. Maybe a lifetime. But God forgives you now, so rest in that.

Grace Is Amazing

When I married Robbie, he was my knight in shining armor. I just *knew* that he was going to fill all our gaps—the love gap, the discipline gap, the play-with-the-kids gap, the romance gap.

But it wasn't long before I discovered that I had married a human, not an angel, and he had his own gaps. He didn't meet my incredibly specific expectations, and I didn't meet his.

My kids were so little that I thought it would be easy! It wasn't. I didn't know what to do. Had I made a mistake? Should I have waited longer to marry? Were my children the issue, or did my husband deserve some of the responsibility?

I worried myself sick trying to figure out our problems. Our blended life wasn't perfect, and I wanted perfect!

I wanted to fix it. "I don't know how to pray, God," I whispered. "I don't know how to heal our family relationships."

Then I realized that I couldn't fix things by myself. I couldn't heal our relationships. It wasn't my job. It was God's job. My role was to show God's grace to my family.

Grace is something I always want for myself. I know I'm going to mess up, so I need patience, do-overs, and forgiveness. I want someone to give me things I don't deserve. That's God's grace in a nutshell. But we also need to extend that same grace to others.

I had to change my expectations. When something or someone made me upset, I needed to take a breath, remind myself that no one's perfect, then deal with the situation.

Blended-family happiness isn't about making things conform to the perfect scenario in your head. It's about the joy that comes when we let go of bitterness and give everyone permission to make mistakes. And when we do fail, it's about the joy that comes when we know forgiveness is available. That's grace.

Earlier I mentioned Ron Deal's statement that, on average, it takes five to seven years for a blended family to bond. This means that some of your children will be teenagers or even adults by the time you start to see each other as "family." Five to seven years of extra grace!

Second Corinthians 8:7 says, "But as you excel in everything—in faith, in speech, in knowledge, in all earnestness, and in our love for you—see that you excel in this act of grace also."

Grace allows us to keep loving each other, giving the best of ourselves, and working to grow together—even when we don't deserve it.

A NEW IDENTITY

AS WE SAT TOGETHER IN A RESTAURANT, David pointed out a couple on the other side of the room. The man and woman sat across the table from each other in silence, staring down at their electronic devices, looking bored and uninterested. They seemed as if they would rather be anywhere else in the world.

"You see those two?" David said. "That will never be us."

He was right. David and I were well suited for each other. We used to joke that we must have been separated at birth. We had a similar sense of humor. No one could make me laugh like he could. We had the same taste in music and movies. We even argued in the same way. We were best friends, and there was no one I would rather spend my time with.

When David died, I mourned his friendship the most. I still do. All the memories we had as a couple—I have no one else to remember them with. Most of them happened before our children were born, so they can't even remember them with me. Boy oh boy, did we have some fun memories!

As a single mom, I wondered, *Will I ever have that again? Is it possible to be best friends with someone else?*

It's the old "soulmate" pursuit. People are always looking for their soulmate. If you've been divorced, it might have crossed your mind that even if your first spouse wasn't your soulmate, then maybe the next one would be. So you found someone else, hoping this time you found the partner of your dreams. And now, perhaps this new person isn't working out as well as you'd hoped. You might be wondering if your soulmate is still out there.

But is a soulmate something you hunt for? Someone you find?

David and I used to counsel a lot of young married couples. In one case, a disgruntled young bride wanted a divorce after only a year of marriage because, as she put it, she "didn't marry her soulmate." David's response was profound. He told her, "A soulmate isn't someone you find. It's someone you intentionally and prayerfully become."

Both of us said that the key to a fulfilling marriage wasn't finding the right person, but *becoming* the right person according to the biblical guidelines for marriage and the notion of *phileo* love—the kind of warmth and affection that seeks to make the other person happy. We believed wholeheartedly that any two serious Christians who obey Scripture and live according to God's principles can have a "soulmate" marriage, no matter how different the two seem.

When David died, I faced my own opportunity to find out if our theory was correct. Could I have another soulmate marriage? Was it true that being a soulmate was something you become?

Today, having experienced a remarriage for myself, I believe we were right.

A second marriage typically requires a lot more effort and tenacity than a first marriage, no matter whom you marry. But "becoming one" still follows the same general process—love God, follow His guidelines, and make your spouse a priority.

Robbie and I don't have the same kind of relationship that David and I did. Sometimes my husband is so quiet that we probably look like that couple David said would "never be us."

But our marriage is just different, not bad. How could it possibly be the same as my first marriage? I've married two different people with completely different personalities, backgrounds, senses of humor, love languages, and everything else. But you know what they do have in common? They both have a deep personal relationship with Jesus Christ, and they both built everything else in their lives on that foundation.

Been There. Done That. Didn't Help.

Even though we both put in the effort to *become* soulmates, I was still surprised by how much work a second marriage takes. I thought it would be easier for us. After all, both of our previous marriages were healthy and loving. That experience, coupled with my many years of work in marriage and family ministry, made me confident that Robbie and I would have a marriage to be envied.

It wasn't long before reality crashed my party.

Neither my previous experience with a wonderful marriage nor my ministry experience made my new marriage easier. I wonder if my past actually made it harder, as I married a new man with a different personality. His children were in different stages of life from mine. These factors, and others, meant that I basically had to learn marriage and family life all over again. It was frustrating to realize I had to start almost from scratch.

I learned very quickly that my previous marriage experience had created ruts in my thoughts and actions. Most of the wisdom, knowledge, and experience I'd gained in my previous relationship didn't apply to a blended family.

I mentioned earlier in the book that it felt like I'd lived in Spain for seven years, only to pack up suddenly and move to Germany. My old rules for communication, interaction, and tradition were all swept aside. Everything seemed different in my new marriage and family. There was no such thing as "This is the way I did it before."

Honestly, it grated on me. For years I had looked forward to the day when life would be "normal" again. I knew some things would be different, but I expected this "new normal" to be somewhat similar. However, it was *nothing* like I expected. I felt out of control.

The chaos, along with disappointment and other emotions, brought out parts of me that I wished weren't there—ugly, unpredictable, insecure parts that seemed to come out of nowhere. Yet the eye-opening process of humiliation, and deepening dependence on God, also gave me a new sense of self-awareness. I became more aware than ever that not only did I need a Savior, I needed Him desperately.

My willingness to become a new soulmate wasn't enough to form a blended family. I also had to discover my place in the family. I had to form a new identity, starting from scratch.

Not everything from my old life had to be erased. I brought much of it with me. After all, our past helps determine who we are in the future. But my identity—nearly all of it—had to change and adapt.

Who Am I Now?

Forming a blended family causes the people in *both* families to endure a type of identity crisis. The roles we used to play in our family of origin have all changed.

The unwritten rules in a biological family first form with the husband and wife. As children are added, they adapt to these rules almost intuitively. When a young couple gets married, they often have at least a couple of kid-free years in which to work out their different roles: Will both of them work? Who will care for children? Who is primarily responsible for which chores? This process can also involve identifying personality traits: Who is the tenderhearted one? Who is the straight talker?

Biological children seem to learn these different roles before they can even talk. Babies figure out quickly which parent is the softy, and which one is the disciplinarian. And as more children are added, there is a type of hierarchy that takes shape—the older take care of the younger.

When families blend, however, members start stepping on each other's roles. Unspoken rules get jumbled and confused. Everyone seems to send and receive mixed signals.

For example, in some families, Mom has always worked outside the home. What happens if Dad marries someone who is primarily a homemaker? It can lead to confusion and maybe even resentment. Like when a stepchild hears, "You can't have that; we don't have enough money," that child might blame the stepmother for not working.

In some families, the older children are expected to help with the younger children. But what if you end up in a situation like my blended family? The oldest child in our house was the baby of the family until we got married. And my son, who used to be the oldest, was now the middle child.

Our experiences in our previous family establish a set of expectations regarding who is expected to do what and how that will be accomplished. And that's not all. Family identity includes other aspects such as personality and worth.

I sometimes think of a person's identity in the family like characters in a sitcom. For example, are you the jokester?

The serious one? Is it your job to pay the bills? Who takes care of the kids? How do you want to be shown love? What contributions do you bring to the family?

We all play various roles in our family, but those roles can change dramatically when you blend your family with another. Maybe you've always loved to cook, but now you discover that the rest of the family likes someone else's cooking better. Maybe you were the one who planned the schedule, but now you find that someone else is better at it. Maybe you were the one who always offered comfort, but now someone else jumps in when it's needed.

That's when you start to wonder, *Who am I now? What purpose do I serve? Does anyone need me?*

You enter a new marriage expecting it to be better in many ways, but you often end up feeling even more broken. No matter how hard you try, the pieces just won't fit. You feel like an outsider in your own home, and you say to yourself, *This situation did not turn out the way I thought it would.*

Don't worry, you're not alone in feeling that way. Blending two families is often a painful process. It's not easy, but it's worth it.

Changes in Your Personal Identity

Forming a new identity in your blended family involves picking and choosing which parts from your past you should bring with you and letting go of those parts that don't belong in your new life.

I'll share some of our blended-family struggles with changing identities.

When I was married to David, my main role was to be his companion. We did everything together. He loved to take us to interesting places and try new experiences. We talked a *lot* about anything and everything, including politics, spiritual growth, hobbies, movies, and music. We discussed our decisions, whether large or small.

He took care of the finances, and I took care of the house. He worked, and I stayed home with the kids. He didn't cook. At all. So even when I made a simple casserole, he thought I was a brilliant chef. It was always the best he'd ever tasted.

When Robbie was married to Kari, he brought home half of the family income. Kari brought in the other half. Robbie was the head chef in their home; he handled much of the cooking.

Kari handled the finances and made most of the major decisions. As part of a military family, she needed to be in charge so the family could carry on while Robbie was away. In their free time, Kari usually read books while Robbie tinkered with his hobbies.

When Robbie and I got married, it wasn't long before our preconceptions about the "correct" roles created tension. For starters, neither of us enjoyed handling the finances. We both left that to our previous spouses. Now one (or both) of us had to do it!

I also had no idea of Robbie's reputation as the best cook in the family. Since I was the one usually making meals before, I put together what I usually did. That's when I started to hear things like "Uh, it's okay. It's just not the way *I* would have made it." That didn't go over too well.

We also clashed over our different love languages. Robbie and I were completely confused about which actions demonstrated love and which ones didn't. I never understood when I could touch him or not. And he never understood why I was always following him around. To him it felt like smothering.

The most difficult identity changes, however, were in our styles of communication. Robbie was used to Kari making financial decisions and handling the details of their schedule, mainly without his input. They were both happy with it that way.

But David and I always discussed everything. There was no way one of us would schedule a vacation without talking to the other first. Or even make dinner plans without seeking the other person's input.

I was willing to assume the responsibility of handling the details, but I was often irritated by Robbie's lack of input. He couldn't even decide on a restaurant! I would ask, "Where do you want to eat?" And he would reply, "I don't know. Wherever you like, sweetheart."

I would ask, "Which one of these dresses do you like better?" And he would reply, "I don't know. Whichever you like, sweetheart."

I would ask, "What do you want to do on vacation?" And he would reply—you guessed it!—"Whatever you like, sweetheart."

There are probably some people reading this right now who are thinking, *That would be amazing! I wish my spouse would let me make all the decisions!* But that's not me. Do you know what *I* hear when he says, "Whatever you want, sweetheart"? In my head it sounds like this:

> *I really don't care about you. That's why I have no opinion, nor do I even wish to devote the energy required to come up with an opinion right now. Don't bother me with questions about our life. I have other things I would rather think about. None of this is important to me.*

Is that interpretation harsh and unwarranted? Yes. Was Robbie really thinking that way? No. But with all Robbie's unexpected responses and my interpretation of them, it wasn't long before I felt like a loser every time I turned around! I started to have thoughts like these:

- *Robbie must think I'm a terrible cook.*
- *Robbie doesn't take me anywhere on the weekends. Doesn't he enjoy my company?*
- *Why do I have to pay the bills and keep up with his schedule? Robbie must think I'm his secretary.*
- *Robbie never discusses anything with me. Does he even care about me?*

All these shifting roles—and my perceptions of the changes—were affecting my identity. I started to wonder,

What purpose do I serve in this relationship? I went from being David's companion to (what I perceived to be) Robbie's burden. I went from being the best cook to (what I perceived as) a disappointment in the kitchen. I went from being an important part of David's decision-making process to (what I perceived as) abandoned by Robbie to crash and burn.

Robbie, of course, had his own struggles. He went from being the primary cook to (what he perceived as) no longer needed in the kitchen. He went from trusting Kari with the decisions to (what he perceived as) constantly being questioned and prodded by me. He went from loving his wife through cooking, mowing the lawn, and fixing the sink to (what he perceived as) unable to satisfy his wife no matter how much he tried.

Robbie and I both struggled because we thought we could just pick up where we left off in our previous marriage. But we were wrong. We had to learn to function in whole new ways with whole new identities.

Redefining Roles

Finding your new identity in a blended family is a refining process. It will likely involve some conflict and frustration as you figure out new ways of doing things. But you can't refine precious metals without fire. You can't sharpen iron without grinding. It's painful, but it's also necessary.

Romans 5:3-5 tells us that we glorify God in our sufferings because suffering produces perseverance, perseverance produces character, and character produces hope. When your blended family seems particularly volatile—kids arguing, spouses bickering, everyone on the verge of losing it—know this is the fire that refines.

A lot of refining occurs against our will, and that's definitely true when it comes to the refining of roles in a blended family. We didn't ask for it, so it's time to batten down the hatches and hold on till the storm passes. But there are some things you can do to help move the process along. Here are a few suggestions.

Discuss your new roles. Remarried couples often overlook the need for this because it happened so naturally in their first marriages. But the simple act of talking about assigning roles can help a blended household function more smoothly, like applying oil to a machine.

Let me give you a real-life example: Being the family chef is part of what made Robbie feel valuable. He loved to hear the rave reviews for his made-from-scratch chicken and dumplings or his perfectly seasoned steaks. His cooking skill was always a major part of his contribution to the family.

When I figured out how important it was to him, everything made sense. So guess who does all our major holiday cooking? Guess who prepares the birthday meals? Robbie! And if I need to whip up a quick casserole some evening, he doesn't critique. There's no longer a need to compete.

We've all had to work through similar issues at some point. I've taken on the finances, for example, and I've learned to make most major decisions without his input. He's learned to speak my love languages and offer *more* input when I ask for it. He thought "Whatever you want, sweetheart," was exactly what I wanted to hear because that's what Kari wanted to hear.

Begin to see yourself in a new way. We get used to a certain way of life. And when that way of life is taken away, we naturally look for a way to get things "back to normal."

But normal is gone and it isn't coming back! You're living the new normal now. Ask yourself: *What can I contribute to this relationship? What roles can I fill?*

You need to dream new dreams. Pursue new goals. Find new ways to contribute that make you feel fulfilled. A new identity starts when you imagine new goals, and new goals give you a refreshed sense of purpose. This new identity gives you something to learn about, to look forward to, and to talk about with others.

As I first got to know Robbie, I asked him about his dreams. What did he still want to do with his life? What were his personal goals? He struggled to come up with any. That's when I knew he hadn't created new dreams for his new life without Kari.

It took Robbie several years into our marriage before he could get excited about his dreams. Nowadays he has so many great schemes up his sleeve that I can barely keep him at home.

You can also dream *with* your spouse. Discuss the things you always wanted to do—then try some of them *together*.

Visit places that neither of you have seen before. Try scratching off some items on your bucket lists as a team.

Learn to treasure the good. Philippians 4:8 says, "Whatever is true, whatever is honorable, whatever is just, whatever is pure, whatever is lovely, whatever is commendable, if there is any excellence, if there is anything worthy of praise, think about these things."

Our thoughts influence our emotions and actions. If you spend your time thinking about all the ways your spouse doesn't appreciate you, you will become depressed and angry, and you'll take it out on your family. In the world of counseling, this is called rumination. Women can be especially bad about replaying negative words and situations in their heads. That's how bitterness creeps in.

Rather than ruminate on the bad, learn to treasure the good that happens in your blended family. Did you do something to make your family proud? Were you able to use one of your new roles to help make family life better? Did one of the stepchildren appreciate something you did? Think about those things.

For some reason, it's easy for us humans to recall all the bad stuff that happens to us; it's usually much harder to remember the good. If you find that the bad constantly outweighs the good in your mind, make a list of the good and keep it nearby. Consult it as often as necessary. Keep adding new items to the list.

I used to keep a one-line-a-day journal. Instead of

journaling about the daily grind, I wrote about one happy memory that I wanted to remember. It might have been something sweet my husband said to me or a funny moment with one of the kids. Keep these happy memories in a Bible, a notebook, or your phone—somewhere you will see it regularly.

Remember that God has a purpose for your life. Being a stepparent is often a thankless job. You handle all the work of a biological parent but receive very little appreciation or validation. But being a stepparent is part of your identity now, and no matter how good you are at your job, some family members will find a reason to blame you!

All of us are susceptible to the trap of "keeping score." It goes something like this: *I can't believe how hard I worked to get exactly what she wanted for Christmas, and I never even got a thank you.* In your mind there is a mental scorecard, and no one in the family will ever score as many points as you. It's a recipe for resentment.

The answer? Don't expect anything in return for your good deeds. Don't expect gratitude. Don't expect validation. Your spouse will never appreciate everything you do in the exact way you want to be appreciated. Your stepchildren will never thank you for everything you do. But God sees every good deed. Do your work unto Him as an offering and you will never feel like a failure.

First Corinthians 15:58 tells us, "My beloved brothers, be steadfast, immovable, always abounding in the work of the

Lord, knowing that in the Lord your labor is not in vain." Every work we do for God is another seed planted. You sow seeds of kindness, love, patience, and goodness every time you do something for your family while seeking nothing in return.

Even if you never receive a word of thanks in this life, God still sees you.

There is no way to please everyone all the time, especially in complicated situations like blended families. There were times when it felt like I was failing every moment of every day. Life in a blended family often feels like a lose-lose situation! If you tell one stepchild to clean up her room, she'll be mad because her parent never asked her to do so. But if you leave her alone and tell the other kids to clean up their rooms, she'll be mad because you left her out. You just can't win!

That's why the words of Galatians 1:10 should be placed where you can see them every day. The passage reads, "Am I now seeking the approval of man, or of God? Or am I trying to please man? If I were still trying to please man, I would not be a servant of Christ."

Only when you seek God's approval will you find the affirmation you long for. And best of all, your identity in Christ never changes. It's the one identity in your blended-family life that you can always hold on to—even when everything else seems to shift beneath you. When you are dizzied by the rapid pace of change in your blended family, close your eyes and hold tight to who God says you are. That's where you'll find peace in the chaos.

Changes to Your Identity as a Couple

Changes to your individual identity are a big part of blended-family life, especially in the beginning. But you also have to be aware of the changes to your identity as a couple. For example, I married into a military family, yet Robbie was already close to retirement when I married him. I never went through the hardest parts of military life, like deployments or transfers. That was Kari's burden to bear.

Being in a military family comes with a sense of identity and pride. It has its own culture, one I had to learn. I considered myself a patriotic person before I married Robbie, but being in a military family made patriotism a more important part of my identity than ever before.

I never really celebrated Memorial Day or Veteran's Day before. Now I make room for family get-togethers or special dinners around those holidays. In order to talk with Robbie about his work, I had to learn the military's language. Ranks, abbreviations, types of weapons—these were a foreign dialect to me. I couldn't understand most of Robbie's jokes when we first got married because they were based on military puns.

A couple's identity will also change based on each individual's stage of life. When Robbie married me, he was approaching the empty-nest stage. But my family was just getting started and came with a couple of preschoolers.

I asked Robbie if he was ready to raise little kids all over again. At the time he said yes; he was still in the throes of fatherhood after all. But a few years later, his youngest son headed off to college, and Robbie retired from the military. That's when Robbie began to realize how different his life would have been without school-aged children.

Robbie started thinking about all the dreams he and Kari used to discuss. If she were still alive, they would now be carefree, going to baseball games and taking frequent trips to Dallas to see their grandbaby.

Yes, Robbie is a grandparent now, but I haven't approached that stage with my own children. Most of Robbie's friends are already empty nesters, but most of mine are not. These issues complicate our identity as a couple, so we have to work through them together.

These are some of the reasons why I keep emphasizing the need to strengthen your marriage. Having a strong marriage will help you shape your identity as a couple, but making time for your relationship isn't always easy with kids in the mix. One practical step is making time for regular date nights. Time spent together (just the two of you) will give you a chance to talk about new hopes, ambitions, and crazy dreams. It's important to discuss your goals and make plans to reach them together.

Another way to forge your identity as a couple is to find opportunities to minister side by side. Our current church pastor was previously an administrator at a Christian organization before he remarried. From his first marriage he knew the value of ministering as a couple, so he wanted a role in which he could minister with his new wife. That's when he became a pastor again.

It was a hard transition for them, but that's the point. Working together through ministry issues can bring a couple closer in ways they would have never experienced if the two of them went their separate ways each day.

You don't have to become a pastor to minister alongside your spouse. You can volunteer with a nonprofit organization together, co-lead a group Bible study, or participate together in a missions project through your church.

Speaking of small group studies, the Bible is an irreplaceable part of your relationship. It's easy to be a part of a small group in your church that studies God's Word together. Small groups also help keep you accountable as a couple, and the friendships you build through them can support both of you in difficult times.

Along those lines, I can't emphasize enough the value of a church community. And in my opinion, I don't think a livestream experience can take the place of in-person church services. Hebrews 10:25 tells us not to neglect meeting together so we can encourage one another. And Matthew 18:20 says, "Where two or three are gathered in my name, there am I among them."

Paul does not mince words regarding the importance of the body of Christ. Not only do other believers offer different gifts and services, but being part of a church community also lets us know that we're not alone in our struggles.

Satan wants us to think that no one else grapples with life like we do. We become ashamed and embarrassed about our battles. We look at other couples and wonder why we don't have a great relationship like they do. But we don't see what's under the surface.

One woman I know said she was part of a small group for three years before she found out that half the group members were in blended families. She thought she and her husband were the only ones! Being part of an open, honest small group reassures us that we're all in this drama called life together.

Changes in a Child's Identity

Adults aren't the only ones who face an identity crisis with the formation of a blended family. One of the hardest challenges for the children is figuring out their place in that family.

Most kids grow up thinking Mom and Dad will always be around—that their parents are the two people they can depend on—but kids in a blended family have lost that childhood innocence that says the world is a happy place with fairy-tale endings. When a parent dies or leaves the family, it brings up a host of questions: *Who else might leave me? Who can I trust to be there for me? Why did God allow this to happen?*

It's a dark, scary situation, one filled with unknowns. And it's even darker and scarier when the children are young. Plus grieving parents are often so immersed in their own quest to stop the bleeding that they neglect to help their kids along.

If you have teenagers, meanwhile, they are already in a stage of adjustment and discovery, trying to understand the changes to their bodies and the emotions that come with growing up. They can struggle even more intensely as their entire world feels turned upside down by a parent remarrying.

I certainly can't cover every issue regarding changes in the identity of children. But the following are some of the most important variables.

Birth Order

There's been a lot of research done on birth order and its impact on identity. (Dr. Kevin Leman has some excellent books on the topic if you want to research further.[1])

A firstborn child usually feels a sense of responsibility for the family. When living with a single parent, the oldest child often becomes the man or woman of the house. These children feel a sense of pride that their parent depends on them and that they have risen to the challenge.

Meanwhile, the youngest in the family—the baby—often feels adored. These children have been taken care of by older siblings and grandparents when Mom or Dad wasn't available. As the last child, he or she is seen as even more precious as time marches on.

So imagine how a big sister feels if she moves in with a family that has a girl who's older than her. She's gone from being the woman of the house to being outranked by another child.

In our family, Seth went from being the baby to being the oldest in our home. (His older brother got married and moved into a home of his own.) Suddenly Seth was expected to be the mature one and help out with his new siblings. It was a complete role reversal—one he was not prepared for—and it required an entirely new mindset. That's a big transition for a fourteen-year-old to make in a short span of time.

Siblings and Gender

A child's gender also makes up a large part of his or her identity. A family with only one daughter might blend with a household of all girls. In that situation, the girl who previously found value in her uniqueness as a female is no longer special. She may feel like her worth has been reduced.

A girl in that same situation may also be used to extra privacy, maybe having her own bedroom or bathroom. But when she moves into a home full of other girls, she might find they are used to sharing clothes, jewelry, and other possessions that were off-limits to her male siblings.

It's much the same for boys. If a boy who had only sisters joins a family with other boys, he might have to start sharing his toys or his bedroom. He might not be used to the rough games the other boys play or their comments about his sisters.

Boys often tend to band together and pick on an outsider. This can be made worse if one of the boys feels threatened by the new stepbrother in any way.

Freedom and Responsibility

As children transition into adult roles, they inevitably take on more responsibilities. Living with a single parent might have required them to make their own dinner after school. Maybe they walked home from school and stayed home alone for a few hours until Mom or Dad got off work.

Kids in these situations typically have more freedom and get to make more decisions. They might get to choose what's for dinner or what to do on the weekends. These kids won't be happy if these freedoms and privileges disappear after a remarriage. They might blame their stepparent for taking them away. Sometimes they blame themselves.

The book *With Those Who Grieve* includes the story of an eight-year-old boy who lost his father. His mother told him to be brave. Grandma told him he needed to be the man of the house.

"I tried," the boy said later, "but I couldn't be my dad."[2]

When the boy's mother remarried, he might have thought, *I couldn't be what my mom needed me to be, so I guess she found someone else.* He might have even felt jealousy toward her new husband who was able (at least in the child's mind) to fill the role that he couldn't.

A blended family works differently from a single-parent home, but most kids don't recognize that on their own. And younger kids, especially, have trouble expressing their feelings. They know they aren't happy, but they can't tell you why. They need guidance and understanding to help them appreciate why their roles have changed.

Sense of Belonging

Home is supposed to be the place where we all *belong*. Your home seems to understand you. The people who live there know your history. They've watched you struggle and mature, and you don't have to explain why you are the way you are or put on a front to impress anyone.

Home is also a place of nostalgia. Time seems to move slower there, and there's a sweet sense of familiarity—the smells, sounds, and images. Pictures on the walls, mementos, ugly figurines—it all might seem like stupid junk collecting dust, but it's still comforting to see those items there on the shelf, right where you expect them to be.

As adults, we love to return home, back to the place we came from. But kids in a blended family can never really go home. Home isn't the same anymore. Not only is Mom or Dad no longer there, but many of those old family possessions are gone. The knickknacks and quirky mementos are either in another house, or—when a parent has died—packed up and stored away.

What's more, during holidays, those times when we all draw near to family, there are virtual strangers in the house—family members from the stepfamily side that look, act, and smell different. During those special times when we expect to be with familiar faces, kids in blended families experience a lost sense of belonging more than ever.

Even as an adult, Robbie struggled with heartbreak when his mother died. When he was finally able to visit his dad and mourn the loss of his mom, Robbie found that nearly every trace of his mother was gone.

Robbie's father was just doing what widowed people do—processing grief in his own way. But Robbie felt like his mom just disappeared. He was never able to "go back home" and say good-bye to her.

It seems like that's what we often do to children who experience the death or divorce of a parent. When *we* get remarried, *we* are ready to say good-bye to that old home and begin a new one. But we rarely give the children a chance to get used to the idea. We take away the other parent's possessions and put them away, while the kids never get to say good-bye.

What's My Name?

Names are another form of belonging. I described in a previous chapter how Robbie and I decided that he should adopt my children. The main reason for that was so they could have our same family name. But we also added my former last name to their middle names.

Perhaps the biggest adjustment for my children was at school. The other kids and teachers were used to calling them Beasley. Their e-mails still had Beasley in the username. It was a little confusing for a few years, but then they changed schools and now everyone knows them by McDonald.

I realize that not everyone can have their children adopted by a new spouse, nor should everyone do that—especially with a living biological father. You might come up with a name that has special meaning, like calling your new family the "Jones-Smith Gang," or hanging a family plaque that reads "Team Johnson-O'Malley." Maybe you land on a bear as the family mascot, so you simply call yourselves the "Bear Bunch." Consider making it something that the whole family works on together.

However you decide to represent your family, remember how important names can be and how they can either divide or unite your blended family.

Helping Children Adjust

I'm concerned that adults don't always have enough patience for kids to adjust to a blended family. We want so badly for our families to mesh that we spend our time telling the kids how they should and shouldn't feel. We want them to do what we want them to do.

Instead, we should let them work through their feelings and give them time to adapt. That means we have to be patient. It also means we have to be okay with *messy*.

Here are a couple of thoughts to help you navigate the blending process as your children find their new identity.

There will be a period of confusion and grief. Blending with another family is hard for kids, no matter the age. It was just as hard for our fourteen-year-old as it was for our five-year-old. So leave room for hurt feelings, crying, and confusion. As the biological parent, make time for some emotional conversations to help your child find his or her place.

Kids need time alone with their biological parent. When a blended family forms, the married couple is like most newlyweds—they want to spend all their time together, and much of that time together *alone*. But to the children, it feels like the caretaking parent has been taken away by his or her new spouse. The kids might feel like outsiders in their own home. It's another kind of emotional loss, and it can cause depression or rebellion in otherwise happy, healthy children.

It's true that the family should never revolve around the children, no matter how needy they are. But they need to be heard, and they need to know that they are still just as important to the biological parent.

Robbie often played golf with Seth on Saturdays to help maintain their bond. Sadly, I was not very wise in those early years of remarriage, so I complained and discouraged their golf outings. I thought they were just trying to get away from me and my little kids. I didn't realize at the time how important it was for them to maintain that tradition. I have regretted my attitude ever since.

Meanwhile, I spent undivided time with my kids every night at bedtime, tucking them in, reading them stories, and asking them about their day. I also asked about their feelings and their fears. And I always assured them of my love *no matter what*.

It's All about Christ

Whether young or old, everyone in a blended family struggles with a similar question: *Who am I now?* So much has changed. No one knows all the unwritten rules. We keep trying to interpret the situation based on how things were before. But that doesn't work because "the way things were before" no longer exists. The chores, the responsibilities, the chain of authority, the expectations—everything is changing all the time. It feels like living on shifting sand.

Thankfully, there is one foundation you can build your blended family on that never changes—the Word of God. Our self-worth is determined by God, not by our role in the family, our spot in the pecking order, or how much we contribute to the household. Our identity in Christ is the source of our value. When a person finds his or her identity in Christ, everything else falls into place.

Romans 5:8 says, "God shows his love for us in that while we were still sinners, Christ died for us." God doesn't measure our value in comparison to other family members or to anyone else. His love for us is not dependent on how well we mesh with our family. He values us because we are His creation, made in His image, and He has chosen to make us part of *His* family.

During the first years of blended-family life, my own children weren't quite sure about their new daddy's love for them. But rather than trying to force a relationship with Robbie or sound like I was not sympathetic to their feelings, I kept reminding them that their ultimate Father was God and that He loved them unconditionally.

Robbie is an imperfect person who makes mistakes. Seth is an older brother who is inevitably going to hurt feelings. And I'm a stepmother, so I'm definitely flawed! Everyone in a blended family, including you, will fail to be the loving people they should be. But God will never fail, will never make a mistake, and will never stop loving us just as we are.

I wanted to establish the truth of God's love in my children's lives when they were still young. So every day when I dropped them off at school, I asked them, "Who does God say you are?" And they would tell me things like "I'm an overcomer," "beloved," "a child of the King," "more than a conqueror," "redeemed," and "called for a purpose."

Finding our purpose in Christ is just as important for adults. We are who we are—filled with failures, broken pasts, differences of thinking, expectations, and so on. And these issues can make us feel like we have nothing more to offer, like we aren't good enough.

I cried my share of tears while trying to find my place in my new, blended-family life. There was a time when I wasn't sure who I was anymore. I felt like my spouse was disappointed in me and my stepchildren were suffering.

In my soul I cried out, *Oh God, I'm lost! Come and find me!* Like a bleating sheep who had wandered off, I pleaded for the Shepherd to come for me, and I knew He would. He promised, "If a man has a hundred sheep, and one of them has gone astray, does he not leave the ninety-nine on the mountains and go in search of the one that went astray?" (Matthew 18:12).

Today the Shepherd reminds me that, through the mercy and the precious blood of Christ, I don't have to work for anyone's favor. I already have the favor of God! When I stop trying to find satisfaction in earthly relationships and instead find my value as a child of God, He fills my cup to overflowing. That same cup spills over and pours out, covering my marriage, my children, and all other relationships in my life.

So who am I now? Well, I'm a jumbled-up mess of a person who is still figuring out how this new life works.

But instead of talking about that part of me, let me tell you who I am in Christ.

I am free. *If the Son sets you free, you will be free indeed* (John 8:36).

I am free from worry, burdens, and guilt—free from the shackles of sin and the death that my sins deserve.

But I'm not just free *from*, I am also free *to*. I'm free to be lighthearted, hope-filled, and encouraged. And I am free to represent the Lord, despite (and even because of) my imperfections.

I am forgiven. *"Come now, let us reason together, says the* LORD: *though your sins are like scarlet, they shall be as white as snow"* (Isaiah 1:18).

I no longer have to carry the guilt for my sins or fear God's wrath. Even when men and women hold a grudge against me, my record before God stands clear.

I am an overcomer. *In all these things we are more than conquerors through him who loved us. For I am sure that neither death nor life, nor angels nor rulers, nor things present nor things* *to come, nor powers, nor height nor depth, nor anything else in all creation, will be able to separate us from the love of God in Christ Jesus our Lord* (Romans 8:37-39).

No matter the battles I face, God has given me the power to overcome and emerge on the other side with riches far greater than anything of earthly value. The treasures God offers never rust or fade, and they never go out of style or lose their luster. They include love, joy, peace, patience, kindness, goodness, faithfulness, gentleness, and self-control (Galatians 5:22-23).

I am created for a purpose. *We are his workmanship, created in Christ Jesus for good works, which God prepared beforehand, that we should walk in them* (Ephesians 2:10).

God created me specifically for a task, not just to sit around complaining about my sorrows and woes. And He planned my role in His Kingdom before I was born! I'm not a nameless face in the masses. No, He fashioned a custom-made plan for my life, including work that matters to the Kingdom. Despite my shortcomings and fears, God uses me.

I am a work in progress. *I am sure of this, that he who began a good work in you will bring it to completion at the day of Jesus Christ* (Philippians 1:6).

Very few verses have comforted me like this last one has in the years since David died. Whenever I get discouraged, this verse reminds me that there are still more wonders to come. My answer to the question *Who am I?* is ever-changing, but who I am in Christ never changes.

Our job is easy if we trust God to do His. All we really need to do is obey the Word of the Lord, from an attitude of love, and watch God do a wonderful work in our lives. We keep our eyes not on ourselves or even on our blended families but on Him.

BROKEN CAN
BE BEAUTIFUL

ALL THIS TALK of death, divorce, remarriage, and blended-family issues can create a sense of foreboding. There is so much brokenness in a blended family—from sorrow and grief to misunderstanding and resentment. A reader might wonder if a blended family can ever be happy.

I liken a blended family to a broken pitcher. Imagine dropping a glass or ceramic pitcher on a concrete slab. It shatters into a million pieces. That's what a tragedy, like death or divorce, can do to a person's heart.

That pitcher will never be the same. Even if it could be glued back together, it won't hold water. But maybe God never meant for your life to be a container. Maybe you were meant for more.

Consider what happens when you sweep up the broken shards and give them to a master artist. He takes those broken pieces, cleans them off, and rearranges them. He devises a plan and places the fragments one by one exactly where he wants them to go. And when he is finished, those broken shards become a beautiful mosaic that tells a story, reflecting the creativity of the master artist.

Our lives are made up of broken pieces, but when we hand them over to God, He makes something special out of the shards. The fact that we're broken doesn't mean we're not beautiful.

Do You Trust Him?

Sometimes my kids want to know all the details of my decisions. When I say they need to wait for something, they immediately want to know why. They haven't had enough life experience to understand all the whys, so sometimes I'll respond, "Can you trust me? Do you know I'm your mother and I want what's best for you? Can you just trust me to know what I'm talking about?"

That's what God is saying to those of us in blended families: *Trust me. I know you. I love you, and I know what's best. You don't have to know all the details.*

Before I met Robbie, I had a David-sized hole in my heart. I had a hard time meeting other men because what I really wanted was what I'd lost. No one would have been the perfect fit because that part of me was broken.

I had to accept the truth that the man I kept looking for was no longer available. He was gone. That realization was what opened my heart up to meet Robbie. Best of all, Robbie was very much alive and was also looking for someone to spend the rest of his life with.

I realized that I had a choice to make. I could either remain true to the man I was looking for—the man who no longer lived—or I could learn to be happy with the man that God brought into my life. Did I trust Him to make something beautiful out of my brokenness?

Thankfully I did!

I Want It, and I Want It Now!

I've said that forming a blended family is like one of those reality TV shows where they put a group of strangers in a remote location to see how they handle life together. At first, everyone is optimistically suspicious. Some form alliances within a couple of days or even hours. Others are almost universally ostracized.

By the end of the show, the viewers have witnessed all sorts of drama. The different personalities clash. Someone is offended by someone else's tone of voice or unusual habits. And all the "little things" in life transform into huge problems! I've never seen a single show where everyone gets along with everyone else.

Yet here in the real world, we put a group of strangers together, call them a family, and expect everyone to start loving each other.

How can *anyone* realistically expect that to happen? Most of us barely know one another!

Maybe it's because we live in a culture that expects instant results—instant coffee, instant oatmeal, instant answers from Google. So when we form a blended family, we expect instant contentment and happiness. Even the term *blended* has a sense of *instant* about it. Food in a blender is instantly mixed.

But as the late minister Paul Billheimer asked in his book *Don't Waste Your Sorrows*, how did the instant foods become instant? It involved precooking—preparation, pressure, heat, and packaging. Nothing is really *instant*. Someone had to do the work at some point.[1]

Forming blended-family relationships means we have to do the work. It requires building trust, finding common ground, and developing respect for each other. It can't be rushed any more than growing the beans for our "instant" coffee.

We remarried couples are eager for stability. We want validation that we made the right decision. We want to know that our children are happy. It seems like sadness follows stepfamilies around, and we're tired of it.

We get frustrated, so we start pushing for an instant family. We don't want to *wait* on God. We want blending, and we want it now!

The last thing we want is for our blended family to open new wounds and create new levels of grief. That's painful to see when we're already so worn out from hurting. We're weary of watching our children suffer. We're tired of worry-ing about and working on relationships.

Worst of all, we thought this new marriage was our little ray of happiness. Instead, it feels like just another knife to the hearts of those who have already endured so much.

Yet the process I've just described is exactly what we must go through for our blended family to heal and to, well, blend.

How Long, O Lord?

Year after year, we watch as things seem to get worse, not better. That's when we start to cry out, "How long, O Lord?" We want a timeline. We want a set date for resolution that we can put on the calendar and fit into our schedules.

Pastor and theologian John Piper, in his book *When the Darkness Will Not Lift*, explains how Christians who cry out to God for deliverance must learn to wait on Him:

> Only God knows how long we must wait. . . . We can draw no deadlines for God. He hastens or he delays as he sees fit. And his timing is all-loving toward his children. Oh, that we might learn to be patient in the hour of darkness. I don't mean that we make peace with darkness. We fight for joy. But we fight as those who are saved by grace and held by Christ.[2]

In his book *When You Lose a Loved One*, author and minister Charles Allen says, "If God says 'No,' we can accept it. If He says 'Yes,' we are glad. But when God keeps saying 'Wait,' we find that hardest to bear. And sometimes it does seem that God waits too long. But He doesn't."[3] Remember that God is a healer (see Exodus 15:26) and that He is near to the brokenhearted (Psalm 34:18). He comforts His people.

There can be very sweet times of mending and connecting with your blended family if you take the time to listen to their pain. As Billheimer wrote, "All affliction is intended to drive one to God."[4] In other words, your pain is not accidental. God can use it to draw you closer to Himself.

It takes patience to wait on the Master Artist. He takes His time, carefully placing every broken piece exactly where it is meant to be. But the wait is worth it.

Building Havilah

It's strange to be part of a family that formed after the death of our loved ones. Our bond as a family is a good thing, but it's the result of something sad. I think that tension is at the heart of the struggle with many blended families.

I have a recurring nightmare that David isn't really dead. He was just hiding from someone or living on a deserted island, and he's coming back to be with his family.

On those nights, I wake up in a panic. My imagination puts me in the position of choosing between the two men I love. Every time I wake from that dream, it's a wonderful relief to know that the decision of who I'll be with for the rest of my life has already been made.

When I first started having these nightmares, I knew I had moved through the final stage of grief—acceptance. I had accepted that Robbie was my husband and a father to my children. Though we were once divided, we are now one family. And we love this family!

In embracing my blended family, I am embracing the brokenness that created it. I can't wish away the past. I can't wish David back with us again. All I can do is value the beautiful mosaic God has made from our pieces. This reminds me again of the words of Charles Allen:

> Sorrows and disappointments come, more to some than others, but to some extent to everyone. But out of the sorrows come lovely and beautiful things. Those we have lost inspire us to grander and nobler living, and, instead of becoming bitter, we become better. And life goes on.[5]

Robbie and I built a new house after a couple of years of marriage. It was clear we needed a home where we all had a part. While it was being built, we had friends and family join us for a time of prayer.

While the house was still only studs and drywall, we passed out markers and had everyone write Scripture passages on the wood, concrete blocks, and flooring. We thanked God for His provision and asked Him to bless our blended family.

When the house was finished, Robbie and Seth could finally get all their belongings out of storage; thus, we filled the house with a combination of *his*, *mine*, and *ours*.

We chose to call our new home *Havilah*, which comes from a Hebrew word with a double meaning: "to writhe in pain" and "to bring forth." The name essentially signifies something beautiful that emerges from pain.

Our Havilah represents the coming together of two broken families. We didn't build our new home to forget the past; we built it to bring new life from the ashes and to celebrate hope.

There was a Havilah in the Bible—long ago near the Garden of Eden, it was the land where the river Pishon flowed, and it was said to be filled with gold and precious jewels.

Our Havilah isn't that much different. We live between two rivers, yet instead of gems, our home is filled with the treasures of everlasting life. And together we all cling to the promise of an eternal future.

Notes

CHAPTER 1 | TWO FUNERALS AND A WEDDING

1. Ron L. Deal, *Dating and the Single Parent* (Bloomington, MN: Bethany House, 2012), 79–94.

CHAPTER 2 | LOSS IN DEATH, LOSS IN REMARRIAGE

1. Doug Manning, *Don't Take My Grief Away: What to Do When You Lose a Loved One* (San Francisco, CA: Harper & Row, 1984), 61–62.
2. Yvonne Ortega, *Moving from Broken to Beautiful through Grief* (Winter Springs, FL: EABooks, 2017), 67.

CHAPTER 3 | REMARRIAGE AND WET FISH

1. Linda Feinberg, *I'm Grieving as Fast as I Can: How Young Widows and Widowers Can Cope and Heal* (Far Hills, NJ: New Horizon, 1994), 80.
2. Bing Crosby, vocalist, "The Second Time Around," lyrics by Sammy Cahn, music by Jimmy van Heusen, recorded August 25, 1960, with orchestra dir. Henry Mancini, MGM Records.
3. Nick Cassavetes, dir., *The Notebook* (New Line Cinema, 2004).
4. Idina Menzel, vocalist, "Let It Go," by Kristen Anderson-Lopez and Robert Lopez, recorded in 2012–2013, track 5 on *Frozen: Original Motion Picture Soundtrack*, Walt Disney Records.
5. Jerry Sittser, *A Grace Disguised: How the Soul Grows through Loss,* rev. ed. (Grand Rapids, MI: Zondervan, 2004), 146.

CHAPTER 4 | MYTHS AND FEARS IN BLENDED FAMILIES

1. Norman Vincent Peale, *The Amazing Results of Positive Thinking* (New York: Touchstone, 2003), 201.

2. Elyse Fitzpatrick and Jessica Thompson, *Answering Your Kids' Toughest Questions: Helping Them Understand Loss, Sin, Tragedies, and Other Hard Topics* (Bloomington, MN: Bethany House, 2014), 44–45.

CHAPTER 5 | THE INVISIBLE FAMILY MEMBER

1. Ron L. Deal, *The Smart Step-Family: Seven Steps to a Healthy Family* (Bloomington, MN: Bethany House, 2002), 101–39.
2. Gary Chapman, *The 5 Love Languages: The Secret to Love That Lasts* (Chicago: Northfield, 2015).
3. Gary Chapman and Ron L. Deal, *Building Love Together in Blended Families: The 5 Love Languages and Becoming Stepfamily Smart* (Chicago: Northfield, 2020).

CHAPTER 6 | A DIFFERENT KIND OF PARENTING

1. Linda Feinberg, *I'm Grieving as Fast as I Can: How Young Widows and Widowers Can Cope and Heal* (Far Hills, NJ: New Horizon, 1994), 100.
2. Laura Petherbridge, spoken at a live event.
3. Robert Bugh, *When the Bottom Drops Out: Finding Grace in the Depths of Disappointment* (Carol Stream, IL: Tyndale House, 2011).
4. Kay Soder-Alderfer, *With Those Who Grieve: Twenty Grief Survivors Share Their Stories of Loss, Pain, and Hope* (Elgin, IL: Lion, 1994), 47–51.
5. William Shakespeare, *Romeo and Juliet* (New York: Dover, 2014), 26.

CHAPTER 7 | PARENTING AND GUILT

1. William and Patricia Coleman, *"Dear God, It Hurts!": Comfort for Those Who Grieve* (Colorado Springs, CO: Vine Books, 2000), 124.
2. Ron L. Deal, *The Smart Step-Family: Seven Steps to a Healthy Family* (Bloomington, MN: Bethany House, 2002), 40.
3. David C. Ribar, "Why Marriage Matters for Child Wellbeing," *The Future of Children*, vol. 25, No. 2, (2015), 11, https://files.eric.ed.gov/fulltext/EJ1079374.pdf.
4. Rob Reiner, dir., *The Princess Bride* (20th Century Fox, 1987).

CHAPTER 8 | HELPING KIDS PROCESS EMOTION

1. James R. White, *Grieving: Your Path Back to Peace* (Bloomington, MN: Bethany House, 1997), 83–84. This sentiment is found in a number of works on grief and seems to have originated with Alan Wolfelt in his book *Helping Children Cope with Grief* (New York: Routledge, 1983).
2. Alicia Skinner Cook and Kevin Ann Oltjenbruns, *Dying and Grieving: Lifespan and Family Perspectives* (New York, NY: Holt, Rinehart and Winston, 1989), 54.

3. *Liv and Maddie*, season 4, episode 3, "Scare-a-Rooney," directed by Wendy Faraone, written by David Tolentino, aired October 14, 2016.

4. Elyse Fitzpatrick and Jessica Thompson, *Answering Your Kids' Toughest Questions: Helping Them Understand Loss, Sin, Tragedies, and Other Hard Topics* (Bloomington, MN: Bethany House, 2014), 41.

5. Fitzpatrick and Thompson, *Answering Your Kids' Toughest Questions*, 43.

6. John W. James and Russell Friedman with Dr. Leslie Landon Matthews, *When Children Grieve: For Adults to Help Children Deal with Death, Divorce, Pet Loss, Moving, and Other Losses* (New York: Harper, 2001), 17–18.

7. Paul E. Billheimer, *Don't Waste Your Sorrows: A Study in Sainthood and Suffering* (Fort Washington, PA: Christian Literature Crusade, 1977), 75.

8. Judith Fabisch, *A Widow's Guide to Living Alone* (Grand Rapids, MI: Zondervan, 1978), 67.

9. Kay Soder-Alderfer, *With Those Who Grieve: Twenty Grief Survivors Share Their Stories of Loss, Pain, and Hope* (Elgin, IL: Lion, 1994), 24–29.

10. Linda Feinberg, *I'm Grieving as Fast as I Can: How Young Widows and Widowers Can Cope and Heal* (Far Hills, NJ: New Horizon, 1994), 89.

11. James, Friedman, and Matthews, *When Children Grieve*, 226.

12. Soder-Alderfer, *With Those Who Grieve*, 50.

13. Soder-Alderfer, *With Those Who Grieve*, 90.

14. Cook and Oltjenbruns, *Dying and Grieving*, 53.

15. Cook and Oltjenbruns, *Dying and Grieving*, 244.

16. James, Friedman, and Matthews, *When Children Grieve*, 9.

CHAPTER 9 | HOME FOR THE HOLIDAYS

1. Lois Mowday Rabey, *When Your Soul Aches: Hope and Help for Women Who Have Lost Their Husbands* (Colorado Springs, CO: Waterbrook, 2000), 13.

2. Kay Soder-Alderfer, *With Those Who Grieve: Twenty Grief Survivors Share Their Stories of Loss, Pain, and Hope* (Elgin, IL: Lion, 1994), 36.

3. Soder-Alderfer, *With Those Who Grieve*, 38–41.

CHAPTER 10 | HANDLING REJECTION: WHEN KIDS DON'T WANT TO BLEND

1. Ron Deal, Blended and Blessed conference, Springfield, MO, April 29, 2017.

2. Judith Fabisch, *A Widow's Guide to Living Alone* (Grand Rapids, MI: Zondervan, 1978), 35.

CHAPTER 11 | A NEW IDENTITY

1. Dr. Kevin Leman, *The Birth Order Book: Why You Are the Way You Are*, revised and updated ed. (Grand Rapids, MI: Revell, 2009).

2. Kay Soder-Alderfer, *With Those Who Grieve: Twenty Grief Survivors Share Their Stories of Loss, Pain, and Hope* (Elgin, IL: Lion, 1994), 67.

CHAPTER 12 | BROKEN CAN BE BEAUTIFUL
1. Paul E. Billheimer, *Don't Waste Your Sorrows: A Study in Sainthood and Suffering* (Fort Washington, PA: Christian Literature Crusade, 1977), 87.
2. John Piper, *When the Darkness Will Not Lift: Doing What We Can while We Wait for God—and Joy* (Wheaton, IL: Crossway, 2006), 36.
3. Charles L. Allen, *When You Lose a Loved One* (Old Tappan, NJ: Fleming H. Revell Company, 1959), 41.
4. Billheimer, *Don't Waste Your Sorrows*, 59.
5. Allen, *When You Lose a Loved One*, 27–28.

HOPE
RESTORED®
A Marriage Intensive Experience

DOES YOUR MARRIAGE NEED HEALING?

HOPE RESTORED INTENSIVES CAN HELP.
Our multi-day counseling intensives provide couples with personalized, biblically based support. Whatever you're going through—infidelity, intimacy issues, communication breakdowns, etc.—you and your spouse can get started on a path toward healing.

Learn more at: **HopeRestored.com or 1-866-875-2915**

© 2023 Focus on the Family

CP1894